This book is to be returned on or before
the last date stamped below.

18 NOV 1994

L 21 JAN 98

18 FEB 91

15 DEC 1994

11 DEC 1992

13 NOV 1996

15 APR 1997

15 JAN 1993

26 FEB 1993

26 JAN 1998

02 APR 1998

26 MAR 1993

23 APR 1999

26 APR 1993

30 MAY 2003

30 MAR 1994

914. 2925EDW   41443

PLATE I The Moelwyn Range from Harlech

Snowdonia

NATIONAL PARK GUIDE NUMBER 2

Edited by
G. Rhys Edwards

Issued for the
Countryside Commission

LONDON
HER MAJESTY'S STATIONERY OFFICE
1973

c

The second edition of this guide-book was prepared by the Countryside Commission in collaboration with the Snowdonia Park Joint Advisory Committee under the editorship of G. Rhys Edwards.

© *Crown copyright 1973*

First published .. *1958*
Second Edition .. *1973*

914. 2925 EDW

I SBN 0 11 700349 2

PREFACE TO THE SECOND EDITION 1973

This Guide was first published in 1958 under the editorship of the late Edmund Vale who also supervised its successive reprintings in 1960, 1963 and 1968. Slight amendments and additions were made to bring it up to date but no major alteration was made to the main text.

After the death of Edmund Vale certain changes were inevitable. Dr Colin Gresham was asked to write on 'Principal Antiquities within the Park' to replace Edmund Vale's contribution while William M. Condry was asked to write on 'The Fauna of the Park' to succeed the late Professor F. W. R. Brambell's study. The sections on climbing and on countrygoing and communications have been merged into a contribution on 'Recreation in the Snowdonia National Park' by John Gittins.

In order to reflect the growing interest in the social and economic life of the Park, new contributions have been commissioned from Professor Huw Morris-Jones and Mrs Katharine Gibbs on 'The People and their Language' and 'The People and their Livelihood'.

An appendix on 'Landscape Trails in the Park' has been added to meet the needs of visitors who wish to explore, with the help of a self-guided trail, the rich variety of landscapes found within the Snowdonia National Park.

Some of the illustrations have been changed to reflect more accurately the changes in landscape and buildings over the past decade while other illustrations have been included to meet the needs of the new contributors. The cover has been changed.

'And I for my part can never conceive how people who live in towns and cities, where neither lambs nor birds are (except in some shop windows), nor growing corn, nor meadow grass, nor even so much as a stick to cut, or a stile to climb and sit upon— how these poor folk get through their lives, without being utterly weary of them, and dying from pure indolence, is a thing that only God knows, if his mercy allows him to think of it.'

R. D. Blackmore, 1825–1900

'It's fine your preparing this splendid countryside for the people, but are you doing anything about preparing the people to make proper use of it?'

H.M. Queen Elizabeth the Queen Mother
to Sir Clough Williams-Ellis
at Penygwryd, 1943.

CONTENTS

ILLUSTRATIONS

PLATES

* Inscriptions (after V. E. Nash-Williams): (*a*) CANTIORI(X) HIC JACIT (V)ENEDOTIS CIVE(S) FUIT (C)ONSOBRINO(S) MA(G)LIT MAGISTRATI. *Cantorix lies here. He was a citizen of Venedos (and) cousin of Maglos the Magistrate.* 'Venedos' is the ancient form of 'Gwynedd'. (*b*) The *Chi-Rho* symbol (for Christos), then—CARAUSIUS HIC JACIT IN HOC CONGERIES LAPIDUM. *Carausius lies here in this heap of stones.* Both 5th-6th century, the former clearly indicating that some relic of Roman administration still remained in force in this corner of the old Empire.

MAPS

ACKNOWLEDGMENT

The most important acknowledgment is to the late Mr Edmund Vale who edited this guide since its first publication in 1958. The measure of my acknowledgment is the extent to which the guide is still substantially his in concept and content. His topographical description of the Park is a classic of its kind which I could not hope to better and, apart from minor amendments to bring it up to date, his contribution is presented as he last wrote it. It is a fitting testimonial to a man who loved the countryside and wrote about it with infectious enthusiasm and accurate observation.

I should like to express my thanks to the Snowdonia Park Joint Advisory Committee and the Countryside Commission for their assistance. I am grateful to Professor T. G. Miller and Professor P. W. Richards for revising their contributions, and to the writers of the five new sections. The Publishers wish to acknowledge their indebtedness to the photographers whose work is reproduced in the plates named below:

Baxter's Studios, Llandudno IV b;
Crown Copyright V a, V b, V c, VII a, XVII a;
K. R. Davidson X b, XI b;
J. C. Flemons XVII b;
E. V. Breeze Jones III a;
E. Emrys Jones XII a, XII b, XIII a;
Ron Jones I (frontispiece), VI, X a, XIV a, XIV b, XV, XVI a;
D. Miller II b;
Derek A. Ratcliffe II a;
Royal Commission on Ancient and Historical Monuments in
    Wales and Monmouthshire IV a, VII b;
Snowdonia Park Joint Advisory Committee IX, XI a, XIII b,
    XVI b;
Ronald Thompson III b;
Ken Wilson VIII.

The cover illustration is of 'Snowdon from Llyn Nantlle' by Richard Wilson, born in 1714 in Penegoes, on the periphery of the present National Park. The painting is now at the Walker Art Gallery, Liverpool, to whom we are grateful for permission to reproduce.

ix

1

Introduction

The part of Wales we now call the Snowdonia National Park has been a natural fortress throughout its history. Though a fortress is usually thought of as a place designed to repel invaders, its walls are just as good at preventing escapes. Snowdonia failed, however, to imprison the glaciers of the ice ages for the marks of their struggle to break out are still clearly revealed on the landscape, but a legacy of that epoch, the alpine plant, has been successfully retained. Sixteen national nature reserves bear witness that Snowdonia has successfuly guarded a varied store of habitats of scientific importance together with their characteristic flora and fauna.

Like any other notable fortress, it holds a fine collection of relics of past human invasions and occupations which started with Neolithic man finding a hard enough stone to make axe-heads for helping him in his endless task of making clearings in the forests. The relics tend to reveal successive movements of peoples or invaders coming from the east, a trend continued today by an inflow of settlers and temporary refuge-seekers from the great conurbations. There was at least one migration of a people who did not see Snowdonia as a last refuge for themselves and their customs. A small dark people came westwards from the Iberian peninsula across the Celtic Sea in search of new lands to settle and develop. As they looked with the hope and excitement of pioneers at the mountains of North Wales rising from the sea, they must have felt the emotions expressed so many centuries later by Hilaire Belloc when he wrote 'there is no corner of Europe that I know which so moves me with the awe and majesty of great things as does this mass of the northern Welsh mountains seen from this corner of their silent sea'. However, they established themselves successfully, and with zest, for their physical descendants may be found in all parts of Wales. Their early burial chambers, stone circles and impressive standing stones are still here along the coasts where they landed and settled. Later on, Celts, Romans, Normans, Plantagenets, all left

1

Snowdonia

their enduring marks for our inspection in a region which became a bastion of Welsh nationhood and a safe home for the Welsh language. Now, as a National Park, it also stands for peace, tranquillity and the birth of a new art—that of managing a remarkable part of the world's surface so that its human and natural resources are put to the best uses for the benefit and pleasure of visitors and inhabitants.

Fortresses, even natural ones, should be viewed first from without to appreciate the formidable challenge they present. One good viewing platform may be found on the gentle slopes between the Conwy valley and the Denbighshire moors where the physical barrier presented to the invader from the east becomes so apparent. Across the flat floor of the Conwy valley the foothills of the Carneddau range rise with forbidding abruptness to reveal ridge after ridge protecting the far, triumphant, upflung keep of Snowdon itself. Another good view is that from Anglesey where the mountain wall rises straight out of the sea near Penmaenmawr and continues in an almost unbroken line along the Carneddau, the Glyder range, the Snowdon massif and the Nantlle hills. Or stand on the southern shore of the Lleyn peninsula and look at the almost castellated outline of the Rhinog range. For another view, go to the foothills of Plynlimon above Eglwysfach to see not only the southerly defences of the National Park but also the physical boundary between North and South Wales. The Dyfi estuary backed by the Tarren range is a defensive line continued in a north-easterly direction by the Aran and then the Berwyn range. Between them these four views provide magnificent evidence of a fastness which is still exciting to penetrate and explore for it has maintained an integrity and a mystery of its own.

Up till quite recently these physical boundaries have made Snowdonia a remote and inaccessible place, a fastness of moor, mountain and deep valleys supplied with roads designed only to serve a scattered population of smallholders to whom the rare visitor, be he naturalist, walker or climber, made an interesting diversion. Even now, away from the new roads and favourite peaks, and especially in unsettled weather, the sense of being alone in wild country is still very real and can be felt in a wide variety of habitats and elevations. There is also the magical impression of being among huge mountains which is difficult to explain when the highest point is a mere 3,560 feet above sea-level. Yet these hills look like real mountains. It may be a quality of the light, the deepness of the valleys, the bare slopes which give no standard of measure, or perhaps the rough look left by the mauling of the glaciers.

Mountains are, of course, a source of wealth. As well as the wealth which enriches the spirit by arousing a sense of wildness, freedom, awe, solitude and challenge, they also provide material wealth. They can be used as summer grazing grounds for sheep, cattle and ponies; grow reserves of timber in an island largely denuded over the centuries of its forests; and they can store water and power in enormous quantities. For residents, it is the physical potential which offers a year-round livelihood. Snowdonia is both a refuge and a store-house; mineral wealth is part of the store. For 2,000 years its minerals have been crudely excavated. Old quarry and mine workings with their attendant spoil tips are part of a landscape which betray man as an energetic mole leaving hills not of well-worked soil but of intractable and sometimes poisonous waste. Does mineral extraction under the strict control of planners and amenity-conscious mining engineers promise a more civilised scene in future workings? Yet the quality of the landscape, despite the tips, draws in the tourists. Although there is now more of a year-round use for environmental and physical education, the visitor generates an industry which is only active for a brief summer season of two to three months. It is upon these traditional assets that the mountain economy depends and consequently the well-being of its inhabitants.

For the visitor new to Snowdonia a frequent response is one of astonishment at finding such superb scenery of such variety in so comparatively small an area. Overseas visitors still tend to say that they visited the region by accident and ask reproachfully why we keep so quiet about our spectacular and historic countryside. They say they had never heard of Snowdonia nor even of Wales until they happened to chance upon it. But they are more than pleased with their discovery. The area is well enough known to the peoples of this island yet its failure to be established in the imagination or consciousness of the rest of the world is probably due not to lack of effort by the Wales Tourist Board but to the lack of a major literary figure which makes London, Stratford, the Lake District and Scotland the main tourist trail of the overseas visitor. For some strange reason we can boast no Shakespeare, Wordsworth, or Sir Walter Scott to interpret the significance of Wales. Till he comes, the Snowdonia National Park must be left to speak for itself.

2

Exploring the Park

EDMUND VALE

Snowdonia

NOTES ON THE FOLLOWING TEXT

The abbreviation M. is used to indicate a reference to the one-inch Ordnance map. Distances for cross-country routes are taken from the map with a little more allowance for ups and downs than the cartographer's 'horizontal equivalent' but, as they are not measured on the ground, they are bound to be rough and a little optimistic. The expression *mountain gate* means the gate through the last wall of the enclosed lower lands on to the open mountain.

In spite of what is said about Welsh being a purely phonetic language there is some discrepancy in the spelling of place-names. There is an old established traditional spelling and recently there has been introduced an amended orthography based on recommendations of the Board of Celtic Studies. These are not in universal use, though some have been adopted in official quarters. There are several divergences between older texts and the most recent issues, which will make things still more difficult for the non-Welsh visitor. In my own renderings I have tried to make as fair an adjustment as possible while deferring to my contributors (two of them good Welshmen) and mainly following their preferences. The names of rivers, mountains and topographical features are by no means all Welsh (Brythonic), some are blended from earlier stocks. A large part of Wales was inhabited by an Urse-speaking people until the 5th century A.D. (users of the ogam script), when, it seems, they were dislodged by Cunedda and his Brythonic tribesmen who swept down in a huge migration from the neighbourhood of the Firth of Forth. Those 'hut-circles' which mark so many early settlements are still called, as by ancestral memory, 'Cytiau Gwyddelod' (Irishmen's huts). There seem, too, to be some lingering relics of the lost languages of the Ages of Bronze and Stone.

4

The Carnedd Range

The name is chosen for convenience from the two highest mountains in the group, *Carnedd Llewelyn* (3,485 feet, next highest to Snowdon) and *Carnedd Dafydd* (3,424 feet). They are of particular interest among the mountains with personal names as they are quite obviously called after the last native Prince of Wales and his brother. Other summits over 3,000 feet are *Foel Grach* (3,195 feet) and *Foel Fras* (3,091 feet). All these hill-tops lie roughly in a line north and south with long intervals of high ground in between them. They form the backbone of the range. It is about five miles from Carnedd Dafydd to Foel Fras—all on the skyline, with long views on either hand.

Most of the *lakes* in the group have been appropriated for reservoirs of power or supply. *Cowlyd* is the largest. It supplies Colwyn Bay with water and is linked by an open leat with *Llugwy* and by tunnel with *Eigiau*. It holds some of the largest trout though they are hardly to be lured except by live bait. Over it stands a mountain with such a sharply-cut profile that it can be picked out at once from as far off as Llandudno Junction. It is called appropriately *Pen Llithrig y Wrach*—the Witch's Slide. *Dulyn* (the Black Lake) lies under towering and impressive crags. It sends water to Llandudno, and *Llyn Anafon* (lovely, and quite untamed until lately) now sends water to Llanfairfechan. *Crafnant* is one of the most charming and little altered from its natural self, though the scrub oak woodland that once enhanced it has been replaced by coniferous plantations. *Ffynnon Lloer* is still a wild lake, untouched and unspoilt.

CROSS-COUNTRY WALKS

Along the length of the range from Nant Ffrancon to Llanfairfechan. You must first get up Carnedd Dafydd. The ascent from Tal Llyn Ogwen Farm, at the upper end of Ogwen Lake, should not be used. Make the ascent from the bottom end of Llyn Ogwen up the steep slopes of Pen yr Ole Wen. Between Carnedd Dafydd and Carnedd Llewelyn you will walk above the edge of the great precipice of Ysgolion Duon—the Black Ladders, one of the outstanding scenic features of the group—and then keep the high ground all the way to Foel Fras. From there you can see Llyn Anafon (or Aber Lake) lying below in the northern hollow and find your way down to it or the lower Anafon valley where there is a clear track to Llanfairfechan. The walk is about 13 miles.

Across the range. There is a footpath across the broadest part of the range indicated on M. It follows an old packhorse track from Bwlch y Gaer Farm, Llanbedr y Cennin, to Bronnyddisaf Farm at the far corner of the range, with branches to Aber and Llanllechid. This passes the interesting Celtic fort of Pen y Gaer (page 73) and crosses the high ridge just south of Foel Fras. The walk is about 11 miles.

The Roman road from Caerhun (Kanovium) to Caernarvon (Segontium) is followed from either Llanbedr y Cennin or Ro Wen. At the gate to the open mountain it becomes a green track which is well marked all the way to Aber. It crosses the range at the Gap of Two Stones (Bwlch y Ddeufaen) between Drosgl (2,036 feet) and Tal y Fan (2,000 feet). The *Two Stones* are prehistoric monoliths of indeterminable date. There is a *stone circle* in a field near the mountain gate on the south side of the track (not very conspicuous) and the *cromlech* called Maen y Bardd (the Bard's Stone) (Plate IV b) a little way from the mountain gate on the Ro Wen side. Three Roman milestones have been discovered on this part of the road.

The green track ends at a gate into the lane leading down to Aber village, about a mile and a half away, where it joins the coast road. By the bridge where the lane crosses the Anafon river a footpath leads to the *waterfalls* of the tributary, Afon Goch. The lower fall, a 60-foot drop, is an old tourist favourite. Near the junction of the lane and main road is a green mound, a relic of the *motte-and-bailey castle* of Llewelyn the Great whose wife was Joan, natural daughter of King John. The distance from Ro Wen to Aber is about nine miles.

Between Capel Curig and Trefriw. From Capel Curig a footpath leads over the open moorland to the head of the deep cwm in which lies *Crafnant Lake*, giving a fine view overlooking it before descending to its shore. From the lake there is a road down to Trefriw. A footpath links Crafnant and its rather plainer sister, *Geirionydd* (about a mile to the east). Half-way between Betws y Coed and Capel Curig, by Ty Hyll (Ugly House) and the main road bridge over the Llugwy, is a rough road which leads direct to Llyn Geirionydd and thence to Trefriw (its church noted below). By making a slight deviation on the way down one comes to the still older and more interesting parish church of *Llanrhychwyn*. From here a footpath leads to Llanrwst.

SURROUNDINGS

The eastern side of the range is bounded by the *Conwy valley*

The Maps

The maps following this page have been specially prepared for the Guide by Mr. M. Kielsa. They give all locations mentioned in the text, either by name or by one of the conventional signs given below. The area has been divided into four sections. Places of historic interest are noted by Old English script.

The Editor would like to thank the cartographer for the great care and trouble he has taken in preparing these maps—with such excellent results in clarity and art.

KEY

Boundary of National Park .... ●●●●●●

County boundaries .... ●—●—●—●

Places of interest (historical or other) .... ◆

Landscape trails .... ⬦T

Nature Conservancy .... [NNR]

National Trust .... ⬚NT⬚

Youth Hostels .... ▽

0 ——————————————— 5 miles

0 ——————————————— 8 kilometres

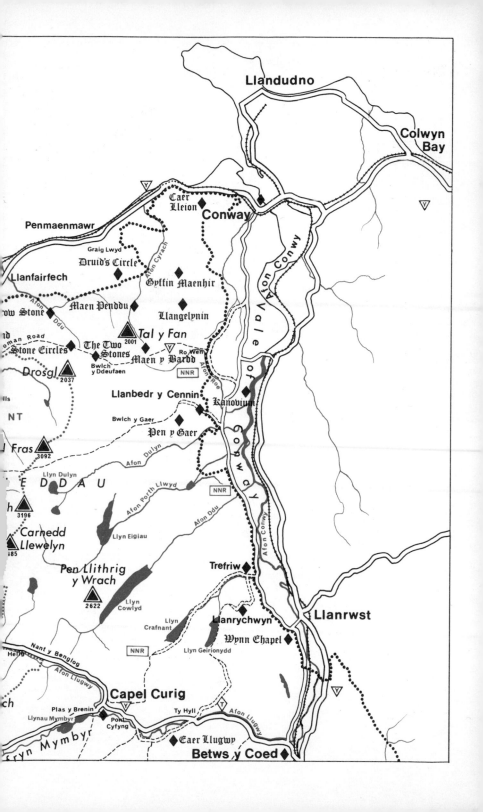

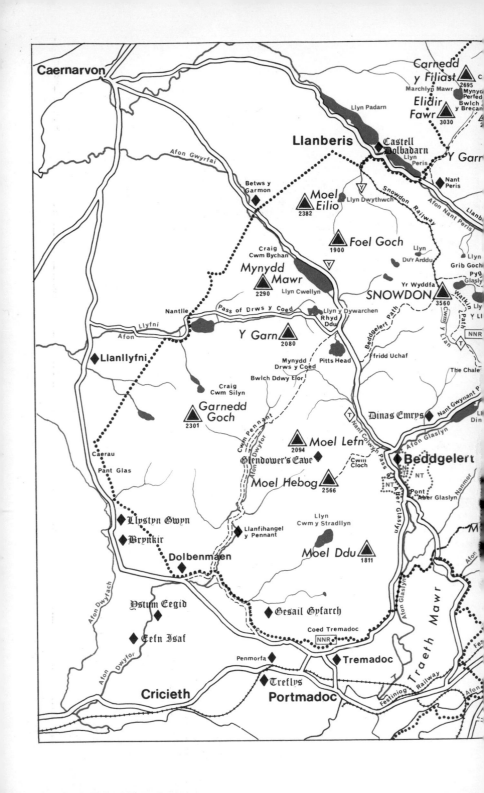

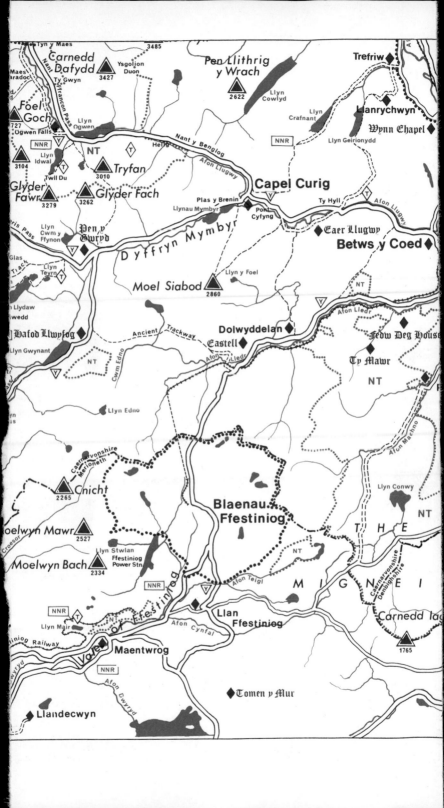

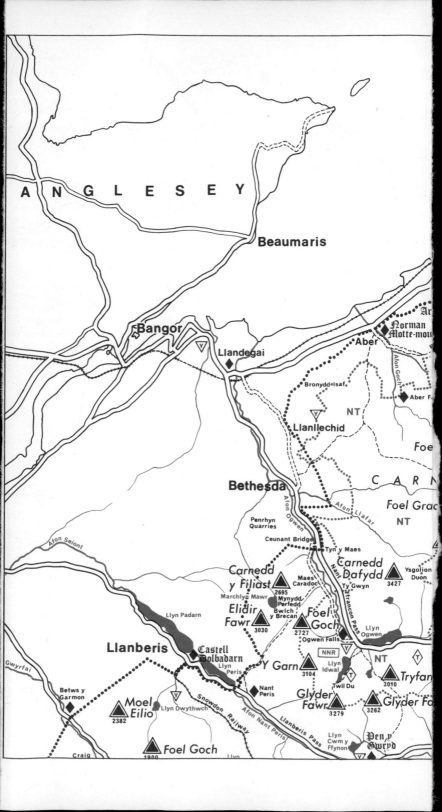

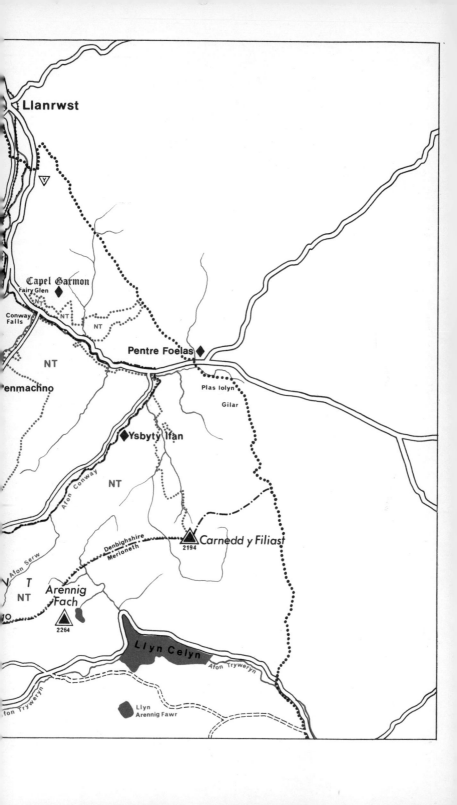

from which it rises with a steep almost cliff-like front making the formidable military barrier which for so long preserved the independence of Upper Gwynedd. Its boundary rested on this line, as also does that of the National Park. The *Roman road* from Carmarthen (called *Sarn Helen*) comes down the valley to Caerhun, where it joined the road from Chester to Caernarvon at the fort of *Kanovium* whose ramparts are still plain to be seen.

The south-west is skirted from Betws y Coed to Bangor by Telford's Holyhead road (A5) which follows the Llugwy valley through Capel Curig up into Nant y Benglog, then through the Pass of Nant Ffrancon and down that valley (watered by the River Ogwen) to the sea. About half-way between Betws y Coed and Capel Curig is another Roman fort whose presence (though suspected earlier) was only proved in 1920 when excavations were undertaken. As its Roman name could not be traced it was given a new one and called Caer Llugwy.* It lies between the main road bridge and the next one upstream, Pont Cyfyng, on the right bank of the river, by the side road connecting the two bridges, which is a portion of the turnpike way made in 1805 before Telford's road was constructed. The earthwork ramparts are fairly well marked. Most of the finds of the 1920–22 excavation are in the Museum of Welsh Archaeology at Bangor.

On the northern front of the range, overlooking the sea, the Park boundary lies mainly along the higher ground and only descends to touch the coast road for a short distance at Aber. At Penmaenmawr, it runs nearly two miles inland and the well-known *Druid's Circle* (now ascribed to the Bronze Age) is just outside it. On these wide open moors a great many prehistoric remains lie scattered, among them the enigmatic *arrow-stones*. These are boulders marked by grooves which look exactly like those so often seen outside old churches and other medieval buildings. They are clearly the result of sharpening implements of some kind, though exactly what sort has never been decided. But prehistoric examples are very rare and, in Wales, seem to be confined to the northern fringe of this range. A fair guess would be that they were associated with the large industry of weapon production from the local igneous rock at Graig Lwyd (Penmaenmawr) established in late Neolithic times.† The finest of

* So marked on M., but not on the Ordnance Map of Roman Britain, where it is called after the farm, Bryn y Gefeiliau.

† The best account of arrow-stones is in *The Heart of Northern Wales* by W. Bezant Lowe. For Graig Lwyd industry, *Caernarvonshire* Vol. I, Royal Commission on Ancient Monuments.

E

these arrow-stones is on a boulder-strewn bit of waste ground a quarter of a mile south of Cammarnaint Farm, above Llanfair-fechan—a large flat rock, eight feet long with more than a hundred cuts on the top. It is just within the Park boundary.

The following *old churches*, within or just oustide the Park, are interesting. *Conwy* and *Llanrwst* have fine rood-screens—the latter, complete with loft. At Llanrwst, the Wynns of Gwydir Castle built two private chapels, one attached to the parish church (1633), another at Upper Gwydir (1673). The latter is intact with its contemporary furniture. *Llanrhychwyn* (700 feet) has already been mentioned; *Llangelynnin*, at the north-east corner of the Park, is still higher up (900 feet) and more out of the way. Both are 6th-century foundations, a time when, no doubt, the uplands were still populated. *Caerhun* church is placed within the (then) protected area of the Roman fort of Kanovium. *Llanbedr y Cennin* has the same charm of simplicity as the foregoing and so has the older church at *Capel Curig*. *Trefriw* has an excellent medieval roof and a remarkable pulpit. *Llandegai* contains the tomb of Archbishop Williams and his monument with the helmet he is believed to have worn at the siege of Conwy (1645).

Knights who fought under the Black Prince in the French wars of Edward III have effigies at Llanrwst and *Betws y Coed*. The effigy at Betws y Coed has interesting links with past and present. It represents Grufyd ap Davyd Goch* (a grandson of the unfortunate Prince David, the brother of Llewelyn the last native Prince of Wales). This knight lived at *Fedw Deg* (pron. Vedoo Dayg) on the hill above the junction of the rivers Lledr and Conwy. The ruin of a 16th-century house standing on the older foundation, and adjoining the farm of the same name shown on our map, has in recent years been put into a state of preservation and its woodwork renovated by the then Ministry of Works. On the hillside, below the present road to the farm, are the remains of the ancient approach by *horse-steps*, similar to the Roman Steps at Cwm Bychan (page 31), traceable in places though much decayed. This is still known locally as *Llwybr Gruffydd ap Dafydd Goch* (The Path of Griffith, son of Red David).

The Denbighshire Portion of the Park

This is shaped roughly like the segment of an orange, the curved part being the right bank of the Conwy from Pentrefoelas to a point between Betws y Coed and Llanrwst where the river

* Contemporary spelling (14th century) as on tomb.

makes a turn from the middle flat ground towards the escarpment on the western side of the valley and passes under the railway line. At this bridge the boundary of the Park strikes eastward till it touches the old coach road from Llanrwst to Pentrefoelas, following that road (the straight side of the segment) to the latter place.

All that part lies in Denbighshire, on the fringe of the Hiraethog Hills, a wide range extending between the Conwy valley and the Vale of Clwyd, its higher ground a wild open region of grass moors and lakes. But this countryside within the Park has long since been tamed or partly tamed. With its numerous small hills and streams (and a farm in every hollow), it is laced with lanes, tracks and footpaths and delightful to explore on foot, a strong sense of the half-wild still clinging to its scenery.

In the middle of the district is the principal village, Capel Garmon, near which is the *Capel Garmon Cromlech*, the remains of a long barrow which was put into a state of preservation by the Office of Works in 1924. It consists of three burial chambers approached by a passage from a point midway along the side of the (former) mound. The original mound which covered the barrow was surrounded by a stone curb which was cleared during the excavation and is now plainly seen on the turf. It shows the indented or 'horned' feature at the broader end, thought to be either a false entrance or ritual shrine. Only the western chamber retains its covering capstone. An earlier explorer of the tomb found this chamber converted into a stable with a wooden door and stone manger. The long mound had been composed of loose stones and not earth, and the antiquary, Edward Lhwyd, visiting it in 1699 compared it with the long cairns of Hengwm which still retain much of their covering. A further note on the Denbighshire portion is on page 33.

The Glyder Range

As seen on the map, this range looks not unlike a Christmas stocking, with the Pass of Nant Ffrancon at the instep, the Pass of Llanberis at the back of the heel, and the wider valley of Nant y Gwryd at the sole. It is formed by a continuous ridge which rises in altitude from the Bethesda slate quarries in the north to a level platform occupied by a small shallow lake called *Llyn y Cwn*—the Lake of Dogs. This is rather like the landing on a staircase, giving pause and forming a turning-point. Beyond it the ground rises abruptly towards the highest point, *Glyder Fawr* (3,279 feet) just a thousand feet above the lake, and at the same time the ridge turns through almost a right angle towards the east. This point is what I have called the 'instep' and, scenically, it may be called the most eventful corner in North Wales.

The stream flowing out of this little lake falls into the extraordinary chasm called Twll Du—the Black Hole—more widely known as the *Devil's Kitchen*. The most striking vision of the cleft is to be had from the point where the stream is engulfed. From here one looks down through the gap to Llyn Idwal again, just a thousand feet below. The whole ridge facing this way, that is, overlooking Nant Ffrancon and Nant y Benglog, is scalloped with hollows gouged out during the Ice Age with their lower lips well above the valley bottom and therefore called by geologists 'hanging valleys'. The rock bastions dividing them are surmounted by moderate peaks, rather in the manner of flying buttresses topped by pinnacles. This makes one of the distinctive features of Nant Ffrancon Pass.

So much is the Ice Age in Britain now taken for granted that it is hard to believe that little more than a century ago such a condition was not even suspected by the leading geologists. Darwin, recalling his visit to Nant Ffrancon with Professor Adam Sedgwick in 1831, wrote 'We spent many hours in Cwm Idwal, examining all the rocks with extreme care, as Sedgwick was anxious to find fossils in them; but neither of us saw a trace of the wonderful glacial phenomena all around us; we did not notice the plainly scored rocks, the perched boulders, the lateral and terminal moraines. Yet these phenomena are so conspicuous that, as I declared in a paper published many years afterwards in the *Philosophical Magazine*, a house burnt down by fire did not tell its story more plainly than did this valley.' But Sedgwick refused to believe in the glacial theory to the end of his days—which were not numbered until 1873.

Cwm Idwal remains one of the most perfect testaments to that remote prehistoric time before human records began to be made. Not only are all those evidences noted by Darwin preserved with quite incredible freshness but there is actually a living link in the shape of a rare alpine flora which followed the retreating ice up into its last high strongholds and has never died out. This great natural museum is now protected as a Nature Reserve and under the care of an officially appointed warden. It is not only the plant robber who menaces conservation here but also the less-suspected rock climber who in times past has scarified rock surfaces indiscriminately and denuded whole ledges of their moss and mountain turf canopies. This is worse than tearing pages out of a book, for replenishment may take long ages and the same story will never be repeated.

In the Museum of Geology at South Kensington there is a model showing an attempted restoration of Nant Ffrancon as it appeared in the Ice Age. The main glacier is seen to be issuing from Cwm Idwal and grinding down Nant Ffrancon above which those hanging valleys are each generating a glacier of their own. The most perfect specimen of the latter is Cwm Graianog. Its floor has been deeply cleft by its glacier, but this gash has been filled by a debris of loose stones on the retreat of the ice, so that the valley has now a saucer-like floor with a moraine forming a neat semicircular rim as regular as a prehistoric earthwork. But the stream which rises there follows the old rock channel under the loose stones and gushes out far below the lip of the moraine. The comely shape of this moraine has earned it the name (in Welsh) of the Maiden's Arm.

The whole range can be traversed from end to end without difficulty. It takes the best part of a day and if you hug the sky-line by skirting the edge of all the cwms and topping all the eminences it can hardly be less than 15 miles. The Penrhyn slate quarries occupy the extreme northern tip of the ridge which one must outflank either to the west or east. The latter gives the easier access. You leave the main road at the lower end of Nant Ffrancon and cross the Ogwen at Ceunant bridge. Following this old road (called Roman, but actually constructed in the latter part of the 18th century to facilitate the passage to Westminster of Irish M.Ps.) to the gate at the fenced portion, a stile, immediately to the right of the gate, puts you down on the open mountain. From here, by keeping well to the right of the stream, you reach the crest of the ridge overlooking Cwm Ceunant, the first of the series of hollows. *Cwm Graianog* is the next one. Its northern buttress is dominated by *Carnedd y Filiast* (2,694 feet) and looking down into the hollow there is another interesting thing to be seen besides the remains of glaciation—and far more ancient. The large smooth slabs of rock forming the buttress are slightly corrugated with gentle undulations. They are fragments of an ancient sea beach where tides ebbed and flowed in that very remote geological time now labelled Upper Cambrian, preserved intact as a huge fossil with ripple marks on the sand, worm casts, and the fern-like trails of marine creatures. Beside this relic of a vanished horizon (now tilted at an angle of 45 degrees) the Ice Age seems a very recent event.

Carnedd y Filiast (The Cairn of the Greyhound bitch) is quickly succeeded by *Mynydd Perfedd* (2,665 feet). Just here there is a cwm on either side of the ridge, which only happens once again—between the Glyders. That on the west contains the shapely lake called Marchlyn (Lake of the Stallion), beyond which stands the peak, *Elidir Fawr* (3,030 feet). This mountain has a very striking profile, like that of the Matterhorn, when seen from the upper slopes of Carnedd Dafydd. At that distance it looks tremendous but the summit is quite easy to reach from Mynydd Perfedd.

In contrast to the escarpment over Nant Ffrancon, a long grassy slope leads down on the reverse side to Nant Peris, beyond which Snowdon stands up majestically and there is a clear view to its summit. The next high point along the ridge is *Foel Goch* (2,727 feet), a fine pyramidal shape as seen from the valley below. Between that point and Mynydd Perfedd there is a gentle dip in the skyline called *Bwlch y Brecan*. The remains of a packhorse track show that this pass was once regularly used as a route between the two valleys. Foel Goch is succeeded by *Y Garn* (3,104 feet) with little *Llyn Clyd* in the hollow below, a lake full of small hungry trout. Then you come to that platform I have called a 'landing' at the instep of the range. Only a little way beyond the great rift of the Devil's Kitchen (up which only the expert climber can venture) there is a cairn marking the beginning of a direct and quite easy way down into Cwm Idwal.

There is a difference of only 17 feet between the *Glyders*, Great and Little (3,279 and 3,262 feet, respectively) and the latter is the more prominent and cuts the more important figure, seen from below. These blunt excrescences composed of rucks of loose weathered grey slabs which send forth moaning sounds in certain winds are quite the wildest and weirdest of the Welsh summits. There is a direct way up from the lower end of Llyn Ogwen to a point between them over the crest of the buttress dividing Cwm Idwal from Cwm Bochlwyd. It is a narrow and rugged way but not beyond any walker, provided his head is not turned by the sweep downwards on either side at one point. From the toothy nature of this reef it is aptly called *Y Gribin*— the Hay-rake.

Clyd, Idwal and Bochlwyd are all wild lakes which have never been tampered with by man. This can also be said of the lonely marsh pool right on the crest of the ridge called *Llyn Caseg Fraith*—Lake of the Dapple-grey Mare (in poetic balance with the Lake of the Stallion at the other extremity of the chain). The 2,500-foot contour runs by the margin. From here one looks down into Cwm Tryfan and towards the great semi-detached peak of that name which rises between it and Cwm Bochlwyd. The summit of *Tryfan* (3,010 feet) is not difficult to reach from the shore of Llyn Bochlwyd, and the shortest way to Bochlwyd is the obvious one beside the fall which issues from it, but the more interesting way is to go up the track from Ogwen Cottage to Llyn Idwal and on to Bochlwyd, first following the stream by the wall. This is a longer round but easier going and you have a lovelier surprise view of the upper lake.

Continuing the walk along the ridge from the Pool of the Dapple-grey Mare it is an easy descent along the gently-falling watershed to Capel Curig, where a bridge on the old disused turnpike road of 1805 takes you over the Afon Llugwy into the village.

WALKS ACROSS THE RANGE

As already mentioned, an old packhorse track (now only traceable in places) winds up from the lower end of Nant Ffrancon to the dip in the skyline called *Bwlch y Brecan*. A more direct approach to the gap is to make your way up the brow behind Maes Caradoc Farm, on the old road, keeping to the right of the stream, when a gate in the wire fence will be found and the open mountain reached. The stream comes from the hollow called *Cwm Perfedd*, a gentle, roomy place, as grassy as its next-door neighbour, Cwm Graianog, is raw and stony. It must have been the pleasantest of all the summer pastures in the old days when the farmer migrated with his beasts to his upland *hafod*. The remains of that house can still be seen. Near it is one of the only two rocking-stones I have ever heard of in Wales. The other, on the Great Orme's Head, which has been a little doctored and had a brass nameplate fixed to it, is not much more impressive. Both are quite small compared with the famous ones of Dartmoor and Cornwall. The Cwm Perfedd specimen probably doesn't weigh much above a ton, but it has had no publicity at all until now, which is a point of interest in its favour.

From Bwlch y Brecan there is a long, smooth, even monotonous descent to Nant Peris with no well-marked path, but the stream is sufficient guide and will bring you down to the village of Old Llanberis.

It has been mentioned that there is an easy way up from Cwm Idwal to the plateau at the foot of Glyder Fawr. It starts from near the bottom of the Devil's Kitchen and is well marked by cairns. From the south side of Glyder Fawr there is an easy way down to *Llyn Cwm y Ffynnon* which is just above the Gorphwysfa Hotel at the head of the pass.

A much less arduous way of crossing the upper part of the range, between Nant Ffrancon and Nant y Benglog, than the rough track up the Gribin is to go from Llyn Bochlwyd to the dip between Glyder Fach and Tryfan. From here a well-marked path can be seen leading round the cliffs of Cwm Tryfan up to the skyline. This brings you out near the pool of Caseg Fraith. There is a path from there to Penygwryd.

On the range itself there are no *antiquities* to point out. Remains of at least two *cists* in Nant y Benglog give a clue to some population in the Bronze Age, while in Nant Ffrancon, in the field behind Saron Chapel at Tyn y Maes, are a pair of faintly marked hut-circles which probably recall a family residence of the Late Iron Age. From that little raised plateau they must have looked out over a birch-wood thicket covering the great flat marsh through which the Ogwen now flows, the stumps of whose trees still remain embedded in the peat.

A most surprising discovery has recently been made at Penygwryd. It is the remains of a large four-square earthwork bestriding both roads just below the point where they fork. It is believed to be of Roman origin—a temporary fort similar to those found near Hadrian's Wall which have been known as 'marching camps'.

Dolbadarn Castle (now under the guardianship of the Department of the Environment) is just outside the Park boundary, which runs between Old and New Llanberis, but the *parish church* is within it. It is mainly a 14th-century building with later additions which have caused it to assume a curious and unusual shape. The framing of the old rood-screen with modern tracery is now at the west end of the church. The well of St. Peris is in a field across the road and was one of the best preserved, having been much visited for healing and wishing down to fairly recent times, but is now suffering from neglect. It is one of those believed to foretell the fulfilment or otherwise of folks' desires by the behaviour of a sacred fish, and various writers, from Pennant in the 18th century downwards, mention the mysterious presence of a trout there. I can verify that when I visited the well in 1947 with a gift of some ground-bait the sacred fish did indeed appear. The old church at Capel Curig is seldom used and generally kept locked (key at the Vicarage at the cross-roads).

PLATE II (a) The Mountain Spiderwort (*Lloydia serotina*)

PLATE II (b) The Purple Saxifrage (*Saxifraga oppositifolia*)

PLATE III (*a*) Pied Fly-catcher inside its nesting box

PLATE III (*b*) Salmon leaping on the Lledr

PLATE IV (*a*) Druid's Circle, Penmaenmawr

PLATE IV (*b*) Maen y Bardd Cromlech

Early Christian monuments, Penmachno

PLATE V (*c*) Llanrhychwyn Church. The small bellcote and aisles under separate roofs are typical of the old Welsh parish church
(*See page vii note for the inscriptions and translations*)

Snowdon

Snowdon is not only the highest, it is also the most distinctive of all the Welsh mountains, and in more ways than one. From the broad platform of Anglesey one may look back over the Menai Straits and see the whole of the northern ranges marshalled along the horizon from Penmaenmawr to the Rivals—a rugged skyline of 34 miles. Snowdon stands in the midst, yet quite detached, its shape more comely than the rest. It looks every inch the complete mountain—there is no mistaking it! Looked at vertically from the air it is seen to be so much more compact in plan than its neighbours—a star-like layout. The summit is centrally placed on a noble peak supported, as it were, by five flying buttresses of rock, three of them knife-edge reefs with precipices on either hand, rising up from the east, southeast, and south-west, the other two extending at greater length to the north-west and north.

This striking configuration gives the mountain a scale of grandeur that makes it appear pre-eminent from distant points of view on all sides, no less than at close quarters and, although in height it only beats Carnedd Llewelyn by a mere 75 feet, the unobscured range of outlook from the top exceeds that of any other summit. No wonder that the Welsh have always regarded Snowdon with a certain mystical reverence—a protective spirit, a symbol of fortitude and long continuance.

The three clefts which give Snowdon its characteristic isolation are the passes of Llanberis (to the east) (Plate XIIa), Nant Gwynant (to the south), and Llyn Cwellyn (to the west). The latter has always lacked a recognized name either in English or, stranger still, in Welsh—for there is hardly an insignificant gap in the hills or the crossing of a watershed which has not been given an individual name as a *bwlch* (pass). So, for that picturesque corridor through the mountains followed by the Caernarvon-Beddgelert road, I borrow the name of its most conspicuous feature which is the large and fair lake, and call it the Pass of Llyn Cwellyn.

THE ASCENTS

It is one of the particular charms of Snowdon that the numerous ways to reach its summit are marked with so much variety both as to scenery and ease in walking. There are at least six beaten tracks, of which the least laborious and, in good summer weather, most completely free of any element of danger or excitement sets forth from *Llanberis*. It is certainly the dullest, but in Victorian times, when Welsh ponies and their attendant boys were available on three of the ascents, it was much the most popular, and the old pony trail is still well marked. In 1896 the Mountain Railway was made. It followed the pony track; and now, if the mists descend, you can follow the railway and be certain of reaching your destination safely. The distance is about five miles.

From **Pen y Pass**, at the head of the Pass of Llanberis, there are three ways to choose from, all beginning opposite the Pen y Pass Youth Hostel. The first is a tolerably well-metalled cart track, made for the copper mines (now disused) about a century and a half ago. It follows a break in the declivity of the southeast face of Snowdon where two lakes lie, the small *Llyn Teyrn* and the large *Llyn Llydaw*, which is over a mile long. On the left, the ground rolls down to the brow overlooking the Pass of Nant Gwynant. Crossing the lake on a causeway, the track comes immediately under the foot of one of those 'knife-edge reefs' just mentioned, which abut on the central peak. Its jagged crest can be seen high in the air and is aptly called *Crib Goch*—the Red Comb. A similar spur, with a theatrically jagged skyline and a still more precipitous face, stands right across the view beyond the head of the lake. This is *Lliwedd*. It abuts on the other side of the peak which, in another moment, can be seen standing very grandly over an upper hollow, from whose lip tumbles a waterfall.

Up to that shelf the track ascends—or what is left of it through long disuse—and there another lake is discovered, *Glaslyn*. Formerly the Welsh, like the ancient Greeks, seemed to have considered the colour green as just a variant of blue and used the same word for both—*glas*. And the water in this lake could well be described by either of those border-line terms, peacock-blue or sea-green. Exactly the same could be said of its river, the Glaslyn, which flows through the pass of that name. That rich veins of copper lace the rocks whence come the springs to fill this lake is plain from the ruins of old mine workings along its shore. Whether this is sufficient to tint the waters I have never been able to find out, but I am certain that it is no mere accident of light or reflection that gives them that vivid colour.

From the far shore of Glaslyn there rises the great precipice, *Clogwyn y Garnedd*, which culminates in the pyramidal peak of the mountain top, over a thousand and a half feet above, that feature that never failed to stir the hearts of bards and patriots, the Summit Rock with its special name *Yr Wyddfa*. The cairn marking the highest 'spot' is just out of sight but its presence is kept in mind through the precipice being called 'of the Cairn' (y Garnedd)—a nice piece of sentiment. The cairn has been so much made up and trampled on that you would hardly recognize it as a sacred site and an ancient monument. Yet the core of it goes back to prehistoric days. In legend it is spoken of as chief of all the cairns on the mountain tops, marking the grave of the most powerful of all the Welsh giants, Rhita Gawr.

To one side of the Clogwyn is a hollow which has rendered possible the cutting of a zig-zag path up to the skyline. If you ascend this it brings you out on the ridge called *Crib y Ddysgl* which is the short link between Crib Goch and *Yr Wyddfa*. This zig-zag path is pretty steep and rough for a man on foot. Yet not a century ago Welsh ponies were regularly carrying tourists up it.

The *Pyg Track** also starts from Pen y Pass a few yards farther to the north than the other. It is a well-marked but rough foot-path and very wet in one place. It takes a line two or three hundred feet above the Miners' Track and brings one directly to the spring of Crib Goch ridge. A clear branch to the right takes one up to the crest of the ridge and so on to Crib y Ddysgl and the Summit. It is rough going but not dangerous in fair weather.

From the turning to the ascent of Crib Goch, the Pyg Track goes on towards Glaslyn. It reaches the hollow about 300 feet above the level of the lake and makes its way round to join the zig-zag path. It is a shorter and wilder approach than the Miners' Track though more arduous. Its chief advantage lies in the views to be had along it, especially those of the great shaggy rock curtain of Lliwedd drawn across the end of Llyn Llydaw, which lies some four or five hundred feet below.

Lliwedd, like Crib Goch, is a knife-edge with a precipice on either hand and a cock's comb crest, along which in the same manner one can walk and scramble. It is easily accessible at its southern end below the lake and affords another means of reaching the Summit. These two ridges, which make a wide embrace about the lakes, form between them what is called *The*

* It is sometimes called the Pig Track because a gap in the spur through which the path goes is called *Bwlch y Moch*. Moch with a long 'o' means 'pigs' but old Welsh had an adverb or adjective 'moch' with a short 'o' (cognate with the Latin 'mox') meaning 'swift, rapid, soon' which would more sensibly allow Bwlch Moch to be translated as 'Short-cut Gap'. 'Pyg' is derived from the initials of Penygwryd whose enthusiastic climbers called it the P.Y.G. track at the start of this century to distinguish it from the Miners' Track.

Horseshoe. To go up one way and come down the other is now
one of the most popular ways of 'doing' Snowdon. But the
elderly stranger who is not in training form is not advised to
try it.

The *Watkin Ascent* (which has the most curious history of all)
starts between the two lakes, Gwynant and Dinas, in the middle
of the Pass of Nant Gwynant. The name has no connection with
the famous Welsh family of Wynnstay but recalls one of the
most magnificent schemers of the Railway Age, Sir Edward
Watkin. The son of a Manchester cotton merchant, he dreamed
of making a railway from Manchester to Paris. In this he nearly
succeeded. By gaining control of existing companies in the north
and south and building a long intervening link on his own
initiative (which later became the Great Central Railway) he
contrived to run his trains from Manchester to Dover and then
set to work on the Channel Tunnel. He had proceeded for nearly
a mile underground on either side of the Straits when a timid
Government stopped his operations. When he was seventy years
of age his tired but still romantic spirit was attracted by the
sublime image of Snowdon. He acquired the choicest of all spots
at its foot and there built The Chalet in the woods between the
lakes and within sound of the waterfalls of Cwm y Llan. It was
natural that after his ambitious projects in transportation he
should wish to provide some means of getting from his own front
door to the top of the mountain. Accordingly, he had a respect-
able path constructed from the South Snowdon slate quarries,
where the cart road ended, to the western side of the Lliwedd
ridge and on through the *Bwlch y Saethau* to join the Beddgelert
path close to the summit.

The Watkin Ascent, though much less frequented than it used
to be, is still the most romantic, rising as it does from a sheltered
valley of luxuriant vegetation, fine trees, thickets of rhododen-
dron, and enchanting waterfalls. The path was opened in 1892
by Sir Edward Watkin's guest, W. E. Gladstone, then Prime
Minister. The spot where he stood to deliver the inaugural
address is duly marked on the rock and on the map.

On the western side of Snowdon there are two well-marked
ways. One is known as the Rhyd Ddu track. The other begins at
Snowdon Ranger, a house opened as an inn in the early 19th
century by a mountain guide who gave it this unique sign and
doubtless blazed the original trail. Later it became a monastery
and is now a youth hostel. *The Snowdon Ranger Path* is the
easier of the two to walk and the less sensational. The Rhyd Ddu

Track starts from the car park at Rhyd Ddu and reserves a thrill for the walker at the end of his journey when it follows a third knife-edge ridge having a long steep descent on either side.

On any day of the year, no matter what the season or the weather, it is seldom that one is quite alone on any of the foregoing trails. But off these well-beaten routes there is much of Snowdon that is unfrequented. Not often is the little, wild, shallow pool, Llyn Glas, which lies deep in the craggy fastnesses of the south-east corner, visited, or the country eastward of the long north-west spur—except the cliffs about the fearsome hollow above Llyn Du'r Arddu, famous for all kinds of rock climbing. But this hollow is the wildest thing on Snowdon. There are two ways across the north-west spur into the Pass of Llanberis, the more direct branching off from the Snowdon Ranger Path and leading to Llanberis through the gap on the south side of *Foel Goch*. The last considerable hill in the spur, *Moel Eilio* (2,363 feet), has always been held to command some of the finest and most interesting views in Wales.

The Pass of Llyn Cwellyn. The group of hills to the west of this pass, when seen from Anglesey, appears like an elephant lying down with its forehead towards Snowdon. The resemblance can still be seen at closer quarters as you approach from Caernarvon. The beast is formed by the mountain *Mynydd Mawr* (2,291 feet) and its head by an astonishing excrescence called *Craig Cwm Bychan*. But it has, from the earliest days of Welsh guide-books, enjoyed the English name of *Elephant Mountain*. Craig Cwm Bychan is a very striking mass of rock and, confronting Moel Eilio, it makes a most impressive portal not only to this pass but also to the Park, whose boundary lies just beyond the church of Betws Garmon (a dedication recalling St. Germanus). Near here is Nant Mill and its garden open to visitors. At Rhyd Ddu a road turns off to go down to the coast through the Pass of *Drws y Coed* between the off-side of the Elephant Mountain and the high ridge that forms the upper limit of the Hebog Range. The watershed is another mile farther on and has a natural landmark in the shape of a huge erratic boulder. In its profile some traveller in the early part of the last century saw a likeness to the then Prime Minister, William Pitt the younger. This gave it notoriety above all other erratics and put it on the map as Pitt's Head.

NANT GWYNANT

The two lakes, Gwynant (Plate XIIIa) and Dinas, formed in the course of the River Glaslyn are the principal features. Their shape and setting among native woodlands and great rock masses of singular beauty give this pass a claim to first rank in natural scenery. It possesses, too, some interesting antiquities. In the upper valley above Llyn Gwynant there is a group of hut-circles —a settlement that may have been in existence when the Romans set about building their fort at the head of the pass, overlooking it; if so, it is not difficult to imagine the feelings of those villagers.

Near Llyn Gwynant is the well-preserved old Welsh homestead, *Hafod Lwyfog*, dated 1638, marking the reconstruction of an earlier house—the one in which Sir John Williams was born, who became goldsmith to James I. He presented his old parish church of Beddgelert with a splendid chalice bearing his name and the date 1610. It is still in use. The house and its land were given to the National Trust in 1938 by Sir Clough Williams-Ellis.

But the most truly romantic thing is the little pointed detached hill below Llyn Dinas called *Dinas Emrys*. It is associated in tradition with Merlin and Vortigern, that unhappy British King of Kent who is credited with being the first to give the land-hungry Anglo-Saxons an excuse for entering Britain. Whether or not Vortigern did beat a retreat to this remote spot, it is true enough that some fine pieces of Late Iron Age equipment have been found here. And whether or not he built a castle here under Merlin's instructions (as the story goes) there are sure signs that some prince of the 12th century certainly did.

Before the old wide estuary of the Glaslyn was reclaimed by the building of the embankment at Porthmadog, shipping could come up to the bridge at Pont Aberglaslyn. Overland routes from here to Caernarvon and Bangor saved weathering the formidable headlands of the Lleyn peninsula and the race in the Sound of Bardsey, and in the Middle Ages, Beddgelert was busy as a seaport. A Celtic monastery was established here in the 6th century. These monks of the native Church were superseded in the late 12th or early 13th century by canons of the Augustinian Order, whose church now serves the parish. It retains two of its ancient features, the fine triple lancet windows at the east end and an arcade on the north side, both of 13th-century work. I think this is not the place to tell or to spoil the story of Gelert's grave.

The Hebog Range

Moel Hebog—the Mountain of the Hawk—(Plate XIIIa) cuts a fine bold figure over Beddgelert and looks twice its measured height.

It is the highest member of the range which is composed of two chains of hills nearly at right angles to each other. From south to north, overlooking the Beddgelert–Caernarvon road, the principals are *Moel Ddu* (1,811 feet), *Moel Hebog* (2,566 feet), *Moel Lefn* (2,094 feet). These are round-headed eminences as their names *moel* (bald) imply—the dumplings of lava and ash from the old Snowdon volcano. Then comes a dip in the skyline where the ancient road into the Pennant valley crossed the ridge at the *Bwlch Ddwy Elor*—the Pass-of-two-biers—and then the great corner-stone, *Mynydd Drws y Coed*, where the range turns to go from east to west.

The pass just mentioned is a tell-tale name, recalling the days when a funeral proceeded from one valley to the other, and the mourners bore their dead on the parish bier up the long rough path to the watershed which divided the parishes. There they were met by a party bringing the bier of their own church to complete the journey.

Mynydd Drws y Coed stands over the village of Rhyd Ddu where the branch road turns off to go down into the Vale of Nantlle through the once thickly-wooded pass which gives its name to the mountain, *Drws y Coed*, the Door of the Wood. The opposite side of the pass is formed by an imposing flank of the Elephant Mountain. Just at the entrance to the defile is the lake, *Llyn Dywarchen*, which has attracted attention at various times since the 12th century (when it was noted by Giraldus Cambrensis) through the freak of possessing a floating island. This only happens when part of the peaty margin detaches itself and drifts off. It is not a regular event and visitors are warned against disappointment.

The aspect of the western chain of heights is as different as possible from the other. Instead of solidly rounded forms it is a series of crests sharply cut round the rims of huge hollows like split craters. *Craig Cwm Silyn* (2,408 feet), the midmost and highest crag, is marked by a large circular cairn which in distant views looks like a round tower.

The range covers a large area whose greatest length is nine miles, and breadth seven. It is penetrated by a single valley which opens at its lowest fringe on the south-west and is closed by a vast, imposing hollow just inside the elbow where the two chains of mountains join. This is the Pennant valley famous for both its beauty and its folklore (for there are families still living here who claim descent from the fairies). Its landscape features are as near perfect as one could imagine. Following up the River

Dwyfor from the entrance, the first note, a dramatic one, is struck by a reef of dark igneous rock which thrusts itself across the way, forcing road and river into a gorge at the foot of which is the tiny church of Llanfihangel y Pennant. Thereafter, the valley opens out to a wide, grassy *ystrad* (strath), and one sees on either hand gentle slopes rising to the heights of those outer escarpments as they converge towards the great precipitous hollow and its dominant peak at the head of the valley and from which its name is drawn—Cwm Pennant. It is a skyline wonderfully balanced (as already observed) by a cresting both round-headed and aquiline.

ASCENT OF MOEL HEBOG

The short way is very straightforward. You take the lane to Cwm Cloch Farm, either by turning into it over the bridge just above Beddgelert or by the branch lane which starts behind the Goat Hotel. Beyond Cwm Cloch the sign on the corner of an outhouse indicates the footpath to the mountain gate, whence you may follow your nose or the numerous cairns right up to the top with only one very modest scramble at a point packed with geological bombs, the well-preserved relics of an ancient volcanic bombardment.

The top, which is quite flat, but punctuated by two cairns, looks out on the opposite side over a long slope, as gentle as the one just climbed was abrupt. A descent on that side, guided by eye, will take you to the Porthmadog–Caernarvon road in about six miles. In doing this you may strike one of the several lane-ends. But to ascend from this side the best approach is to take the road into the Pennant valley and turn off it by the chapel above Llanfihangel y Pennant. Then make for the mountain.

The next eminence to Moel Hebog, on the northern side of the ridge, is an astonishing rock, riven on its eastern face with deep horizontal clefts, the largest of which goes by the name of *Ogof Owain Glyndwr*—Owen Glendower's Cave. There is a strong tradition that the great national hero took refuge here from his English pursuers in one of the difficult intervals of his campaign. Its utter wildness today sustains the romance of the story. Plantations of the Forestry Commission have made it difficult to reach but it can be visited on the third and most attractive of the approaches to Moel Hebog.

This begins at Rhyd Ddu at a right-angled bend in the road to Nantlle, just above the village. There are two iron gates on the left-hand side, the smaller opening on the old footpath to

Cwm Pennant, not used so much as formerly and consequently less well marked. It leads to a small gate in a wall bounding the Forestry Commission plantation across which the track must be followed. It emerges on the high ground and crosses the watershed at the Pass-of-two-biers, descending on the far side of the mountain wall to Cwm Pennant and Dolbenmaen. It is here that you must break off and make your way along the ridge towards Moel Hebog which almost immediately comes into full view.

ANTIQUITIES

The boundary of the Park cuts obliquely across country from Llanberis to a point on the Caernarvon–Criccieth road where it makes a descent to Pant Glas. From thence it follows round the skirt of the Hebog Range and encloses the whole of that interesting region. Near the point (just mentioned) where the Park boundary joins the road there stand three enormous gate-posts. They are re-used prehistoric monoliths (one has been riven to make two posts). The larger was brought from over a mile away within living memory drawn by a team of nine horses. Near them, on land belonging to *Caeran Farm*, is a large settlement of which only a few houses have so far (1972) been excavated, indicating a date of 3rd-4th century A.D. It borders the road, and the old cultivation terraces mounting up the hillside are plainly marked.

This part is rich in prehistoric remains, including the fine cromlechs of Cefn Isaf and Ystum Cegid, but they lie outside the Park. Three early Christian tombstones, all ascribed to the 6th century, are also here. One is at *Llystyn Gwyn Farm*, near Bryncir, only a few yards outside the boundary. It is of particular interest as having an ogam as well as a Latin inscription (the only ogam in North Wales) but it is hard to make out. Another is in Treflys churchyard. The third is at *Gesail Gyfarch* near Penmorfa. This is well within the Park boundary. It lies in the farm garden and commemorates one Cunacus, son of Cunalipus.

There are old parish churches at *Llanllyfni* (with a much-neglected saint's well in a field nearby), *Dolbenmaen,* and *Penmorfa*. The latter, with its saddle-roof lych-gate dated 1698 and memorial to the doughty royalist veteran, Sir John Owen, is the most interesting. By the farm opposite Dolbenmaen church is a large motte mound. This, with its small wooden castle, was probably the seat of the rulers of the district—the Lords of Eifionydd—in the 12th century, before they removed to Criccieth.

F

Tremadog takes its name from that enterprising private person W. A. Madocks who spent his fortune on reclaiming the wide estuary of the Glaslyn by building the sea wall at Porthmadog (completed 1812). The little town with its church, market square and combined market-hall and theatre was all laid out and built by him about 1805.

THE COED TREMADOG (TREMADOC WOOD) NATURE RESERVE

This is situated on the great rocky escarpment which dominates the town and the road leading thence to Beddgelert. It is a dense growth of oak clothing the precipitous face right up to the skyline. Formerly, oak woodland was one of the principal scenic glories of North Wales but in recent years it has suffered greatly either through absolute clearance or replacement by coniferous plantations. Its conservation here where it has always made a particularly important contribution to the landscape will be welcomed by all lovers of natural beauty. Apart from that, the reserve has an interesting botany partly owing to its rock formation and the fact that its steepness has prevented the ubiquitous all-nibbling sheep from reaching ledges where rare plants have had a chance of survival. A *permit* is necessary to enter this reserve. For that, an application should be made to The Nature Conservancy, Penrhos Road, Bangor, Caernarvonshire: Telephone Bangor 2201.

The Siabod and Moelwyn Range

This lies at the feet of all four ranges described—a footstool with its axis at right angles to theirs. It contains two mountains whose features are notable contributions to landscape—*Moel Siabod* in the east and *Cnicht* in the west. Otherwise its distinction lies not in its interior scenery but in the number and beauty of the passes and valleys which it helps both to form and to dominate. Going the round anti-clockwise from Betws y Coed, there is the Llugwy valley (below the Carneddau), Nant y Gwryd (below the Glyder range), Nant Gwynant (below Snowdon), the narrow pass of Aberglaslyn at the foot of Moel Hebog, followed by the wide expanse of Traeth Mawr, the reclaimed estuary, whose sands and channels are replaced by a broad green interlude starred with the gold of gorse; then the well-wooded and rightly-famous Vale of Ffestiniog; then up on to a high pass on the open mountain at a thousand feet properly called Bwlch Gorddinan but now generally known as *Crimea* after the sign of a long-vanished inn.

Down, then, into the lovely Lledr valley; then to a short stretch of the Upper Conwy where, in a deep gap, the bastions of four ranges confront one another, divided by four remarkable valleys. Through one, high up, above the Conwy Falls, Telford's Holyhead road comes and, at one turning, gives the west-bound traveller a sudden and most astonishing view over the deep gap. He sees, as it were, the very essence of Snowdonia at a glance— a highly-modelled foreground of rocks, woods and waters with a broad mountain plinth rising above and, on it, the blue silhouette of Moel Siabod couched like a sharp-featured sphinx. Before the native oak and birch were replaced by conifers this was one of the most wonderful views in the whole of the British Isles.

Moel Siabod is a solitary mountain with smooth, grassy slopes which rise evenly above the Mymbyr Lakes and Nant y Gwryd on its northern flank and its long back sloping upwards from the west, but it presents a rough and rugged front to the south-east, immediately below its summit (2,860 feet). Here it has been hollowed by its old glacier to an amphitheatre filled with relics of that time—round drumlin mounds and a lake, Llyn y Foel, with its island of morainic detritus and large boulders. That 'plinth' just mentioned extends on this side in the form of a large plateau nearly a thousand feet up, from the heights above Betws y Coed to the sources of the Lledr river above Dolwyddelan.

From the Holyhead road, between Capel Curig and Betws y Coed, the mountain is seen to stand boldly against the sky in the form of a pyramid and it is from this side that the most attractive approach is made.

ASCENTS OF MOEL SIABOD

By crossing the River Llugwy at *Pont Cyfyng*, a mile below Capel Curig, you come to a terrace of houses. Behind them is the end of a rough road which served the now disused slate quarries and one or two hill farms. This leads directly to the foot of the mountain on its rough side. It begins by a ridge with curving bands of strongly-marked strata, the intervals forming gullies not difficult to make one's way up and by so doing reach the summit. A more interesting alternative is to continue along the road which leads past the upper quarry with its artificial pools and ruined buildings to the wild lake in the hollow. From here the summit can be reached by making one's way up the middle gully or the boulder-strewn edge of the cirque.

From Capel Curig there is a path up the all-grassy slope which starts opposite the end of the bridge by *Plas y Brenin*. This is now the hostel of the Central Council of Physical Recreation, formerly the Royal Hotel. It was built to serve the earlier turnpike road to Holyhead and opened in 1804. Its window panes bear signatures of Byron, Walter Scott and Queen Victoria. A plantation of the Forestry Commission bestrides the old path which is no longer well marked at the upper end, but by keeping near the wire fence on the right when the trail becomes doubtful a stile on to the open mountain will be found. This is the shortest and easiest way up. Besides the cairn on the summit there is a small circular enclosure. It was a pen for ponies which brought tourists up the mountain in earlier days.

The high plateau, which sweeps round the base of Moel Siabod from a point overlooking the Conwy gorge in the east to another some 10 miles to the west overlooking Gwynant Lake, has a conspicuous building nearly mid-way which can be seen from far off in all directions. This is Dolwyddelan Castle, its rectangular keep reminding one of the peel towers of Scotland and Ireland. Built in the 12th century it is believed on good grounds to have been the birthplace of Llewelyn the Great (1173). In 1488 Maredydd ap Ivan, ancestor of the Wynns of Gwydir, acquired the castle and migrated here from the ancient family home at Gesailgyfarch. He built old *Dolwyddelan church* in the early 16th century, which still preserves its rood screen and some old glass of his time. Maredydd was the grandfather of John Wynn who built Gwydir Castle, Llanrwst, and great-grandfather of the more famous Sir John.

The castle stands near the junction of two ancient routes. Down Cwm Penamnen (opposite the modern village of Dolwyddelan) came the Roman road from Tomen y Mur called Sarn Helen. It must have crossed the plateau to the fort at Caer Llugwy (page 7) though its exact route has not yet been ascertained. From Nant Gwynant came another road which passed under its battlements, but though the direction indicated makes an excellent walk the old trail is now obliterated throughout most of its length. That the plateau was more popular as a resort in both the Iron Age and the Bronze Age is shown by groups of hut-circles and in the eastern part by cist-burials.

South of the old trail, which is like the waist-line of the range, the ground rises towards the extraordinary mountain complex dotted with more than two dozen lakes and tarns, with round-headed *Moelwyn Mawr* (2,527 feet) as chief summit, and sharp-featured *Cnicht* (2,265 feet) the most striking as seen from below.

The best entry into this country, which has a singular charm of its own and commands some unrivalled views, is to branch off the old trail and follow the stream up *Cwm Edno* to the lake of that name. It is rather more than two miles from there to Cnicht and another two miles on to Moelwyn Mawr. Cnicht is actually an elongated ridge, the gable end of which gives it the appearance of a peak from below where, in fact, it resembles the shape of the bassinet helmet of a knight of the 14th century (then spelt cnight and pronounced with a guttural *gh*) so, most likely, it is an English and not a Welsh name given by sailors frequenting the estuary of the Glaslyn before reclamation converted its channels into green pastures.

Meirion
The Rhinog Range

Between Moelwyn, at the end of the Siabod group, and Cader Idris, at the end of the Berwyn chain, is a range of coastal mountains almost at right angles to both and facing squarely to the west. It is generally known by the name of the two sister mountains which confront each other on either side of the principal pass through the middle of the range—Rhinog Fawr (2,362 feet) and Rhinog Fach (2,333 feet). They are not the highest but they are the most distinctive, Rhinog Fawr cutting a tower-like figure with a flat top sloped to the west and snubbed off to the east, the other having a slight sisterly resemblance.

The whole region is markedly different from Snowdonia. The shapes of the mountains, the more luxurious vegetation, the ways of the people all impress one as individual and indigenous. It was, in ancient days, the separate district of Ardudwy, whose chief appears to have had two royal residences, one on the rock of Harlech, the other in the deserted Roman castellum of Tomen y Mur.

The range is particularly well off for lakes, still in their natural state. The most beautiful of these is *Llyn Cwm Bychan* where some fine hardwood timber gives it that touch of richness generally lacking in the mountain lakes of Wales. Other touches are the purple *cwm* rising behind the woodland to the peak of Pen y Clip; the noble Careg y Saeth—Crag of the Arrow—scored with bilberry and heather terraces, standing sheer in the south bank and throwing its shadow and reflection on the water; the single dwelling, an ancient farmstead, for centuries the home of the Lloyds of Cwm Bychan. By contrast, there is *Llyn Hywel*, sunk in between Rhinog Fach and *Y Llethr* (2,475 feet, the highest of the range) the most stark and forbidding of all the mountain tarns in the Park—quite a frightening place!

The hills north of the pass called *Drws Ardudwy*—the Door of Ardudwy—are a compact group with mainly rounded summits rising from a breadth of high ground and culminating in Rhinog Fawr. Their slopes are covered with deep heather, and large expanses of rock-face tend to be lined by ledges and terraces where heather and bilberry grow luxuriantly. Moist hollows are crammed with the fragrant bog myrtle and, in the valleys of the western slopes, ferns flourish abundantly.

South of the pass, characteristics tend to grow more austere, and the main watershed becomes a single elongated ridge stretching from Y Llethr to the headland above Barmouth (some nine miles), embracing on the west side a wide upland plateau, once, and for long, a much-favoured resort of man, for it is covered with the signs of occupation, from the Neolithic period down to the last phase of the Iron Age. From about the middle of this ridge a spur extends due east to the Vale of Ganllwyd forming a watershed which sends a number of streams due south to the Mawddach estuary, their pleasant sunny valleys *Cwm Sylfaen*, *Hirgwm*, *Cwm Mynach*, and *Cwm yr Wnin*, open on the Barmouth–Dolgellau road. The highest point achieved by the spur is Y Garn (2,063 feet).

THE SURROUNDING COUNTRY

In the north, the range is bounded by the famous Vale of Ffestiniog, whose beauty is still enriched by deciduous woodlands through which the River Dwyryd winds down to the village of Maentwrog (Plate XIVa)—the stone of Twrog. That stone is evidently the monolith standing near the tower of the much-modernised church. It recalls the 6th-century missioner, a close companion of the more noted Beuno. The stone bears no inscription and may conceivably have been there when Twrog arrived to found the first Christian church—a prehistoric memorial marking a pagan sacred site.

To the east, the range is completely detached from the neighbouring Migneint by the wide valley which takes such a direct course from north to south that the Ffestiniog–Dolgellau road is almost in a dead straight line for several miles. From the long stretch of open moorland and peat bog the road descends into the thickly-wooded Vale of Ganllwyd (now mainly converted from native timber to conifer), then turns to the west and, at Llanelltyd bridge, meets the tidal waters of the Mawddach estuary. From here to Barmouth the road winds between the shore and the foot of those valleys just mentioned. It is along this southern edge of the range that the gold-bearing reef runs which has been worked by various undertakings with considerable profit, though at the present time all the mines are closed down. Fittingly enough, the scenery along this once tortuous highway has a poetically golden quality, too. Natural woodlands abound, with slopes of heather and gorse intervening; the shore-line is fretted with headlands and sedgy pools; there are constant glimpses across the water towards the majestic front of Cader Idris.

On the western side of the range, the foothills do not rise directly from the shore but form a fringe of low-lying fertile land between which and the sea a long barrier of sandhills projects. To this feature is owed the long-standing name *Dyffryn Ardudwy*, where the normal use of the word 'dyffryn', 'a valley', is extended to convey the meaning of good land between the barrenness of mountain and sea. The name is significant in this particular context, for one may believe that it is intended to include more than that mere fringe of fertile ground. Beyond the first rise above the road there is that ample plateau, mentioned above, which reaches right up into the hills and is bounded by the Llethr Ridge. Except for a couple of mountain farms, far apart from each other, it is only inhabited by sheep. Yet it is strewn with the remains of ancient populations. If you begin exploring at road level you will find a splendid pair of cromlechs in the playground of Dyffryn Ardudwy school. They are the exposed chambers of a Neolithic long barrow which has lost its original covering, but such are the *Carneddau Hengwm*—shown on both the Ordnance Survey and Bartholomew maps. There are other cromlechs in a more ruinous condition. Above Corsygedol you may catch glimpses through the bracken of round cairns in serried ranks—doubtless a large Bronze Age cemetery. Their presence side by side with the larger tombs of the earlier period (the most perfect of the uncovered sort is in the school play-ground at Llanenddwyn, close to the main road) will account for at least a thousand years of settled life in the area. The place was yet again favoured by Celtic immigrants, for there are two Iron Age forts and innumerable hut-circles, which cartographers, glutted by so many 'ancient monuments', have not troubled to mark. That plateau can be likened to nowhere else this side of the Irish Sea but Salisbury Plain.

Probably it was a folk memory of the Old People of Hengwm which started the story of the Cantref y Gwaelod—the Hundred of the Sea-floor—the lost land overwhelmed through neglect of sea dykes, a tale fortified by the presence of an extraordinary submarine barrier of large loose stones extending in a straight line from the sandhills of Morfa Dyffryn for fourteen miles out to sea and called *Sarn Badrig*—Patrick's Causeway. Formerly believed to be artificial, it was an antiquarian problem; now held to be natural, it is one for the geologist, who has not yet produced a convincing solution.

On the north-west fringe of the range there are also prehistoric remains scattered about (many, doubtless, still unrecorded). A by-road going up steeply from Llanfair towards Moel Goedog passes near the group of hut-circles marked on M. as *Muriau'r Gwyddelod*—Walls of the Goidels, i.e. the Irish-speaking people —then, farther on, beside the rough track, three monoliths; *Moel Goedog* itself is crowned by an Iron Age fort. A reminder that these high places were still peopled in the 6th century is the parish church of *Llandecwyn*, founded by the missionary Tegwyn at that time at a height of 500 feet and remote from any modern settlement. On the extreme coastal fringe, too, parishioners have also moved away and *Llandanwg* church is now quite deserted among the outer sandhills, and the old congregation of *Llanfihangel y Traethau* has migrated to newer settlements on the main road, but the church is worth visiting for the charm of its situation and the remarkable 12th-century pillar stone in the graveyard. Of the six other old parish churches, *Llanaber* is the most interesting and architecturally most unusual for Wales, being built in the Early English style, and is complete with clerestory. Two inscribed stones of the 5th or 6th century are preserved there (two of similar date are at Llandanwg). Still more rare is the monolith kept in Llanbedr church with a spiral picked out on it. No one knows who put it there or whence it came, but it can hardly be younger than the Bronze Age. Even more stimulating to conjecture is the much later stone in *Llanelltyd* church (12th century?) which bears the outline of a footprint and an inscription which has been translated as 'The footprint of Kenyric is affixed to the top of the stone and he himself is bound (by his vow made) before he set out on a journey'—a noble pilgrim? a crusader?

PLATE VI The Gate-house, Harlech Castle, late 13th century

PLATE VII (b) Gwydir Castle

PLATE VII (a) The Gate-house, Gilar, dated 1623

PLATE VIII Climbing on Crackstone Rib, Llanberis Pass

PLATE IX Cwm Idwal, looking towards 'Idwal Slabs' on Glyder Fawr

Harlech Castle (Plate VI) has its own excellent guide-book. In the modern church the medieval font of the older mother at Llandanwg will be found.

Barmouth (an old English malaprop for *Aber Maw*) is a very ancient seaport which was still commercially important in the first part of the 19th century when they had found it necessary to build the picturesque round-house on the foreshore as a prison for rowdy mariners. The old town, built so steeply on the rock that the houses have no access by wheeled vehicle, is stranger and foreigner than the much more visited Clovelly. Among the cottages are several held by a trust founded by John Ruskin in 1871, and the first gift to the National Trust was 4½ acres of the headland overlooking the town made over to the nation in 1895, called prophetically The Castle of Light, a beacon to which all National Parks must own guidance.

WALKS OVER THE RANGE

The Pass of Drws Ardudwy is the deepest cleft through the range. Unlike most Welsh passes it is a gloomy place, but a fit setting for the house on the western side, *Maesygarnedd*, and its associations. In the 17th century it was the home of Colonel John Jones who married Catherine, the sister of Oliver Cromwell. He had the misfortune to put his hand to the death-warrant of Charles I and then outlive the Commonwealth regime. At the Restoration he was awarded the traitor's death. On the rocks above the pass one may sometimes see the shaggy form of one or more members of the herd of naturalized goats.

From Cwm Bychan, a paved packhorse trail ascends to a high cleft in the mountain, called *Bwlch Tyddiad*. The path takes the form and bears the traditional name of the Roman Steps (Plate XV). Sceptics name a 17th-century date as more likely for their construction, when the Lloyds of Cwm Bychan were flourishing in the heart of their isolated domain. The mystery will probably remain non-proven, but it is likely that the route is a very ancient one and was not made exclusively for the convenience of Cwm Bychan House, for there are remains of it beyond the farm going in the direction of Harlech, though this part is unused and has fallen entirely into ruin, while the rest is tolerably well preserved. The distance from the farm to the Ffestiniog–Dolgellau road is about six miles. The farmers attending fairs and sheepdog trials at Trawsfynydd have formed an alternative path which goes up through the head of the cwm and leads to the footbridge near the end of the hydro-electric reservoir.

The Roman Steps also provide an easy and attractive way to reach the summit of Rhinog Fawr (the general favourite, though not the highest of the range). They may be left shortly before the *Bwlch* is reached and the way over the open moorland is obvious and straightforward.

The old road from Dolgellau to Harlech surveyed by John Ogilby for his map published in 1675 turns off the present main road at Bontddu. It is metalled and maintained for about two miles and then becomes a mere track. This divides where an ancient milestone of Stuart date (it is shown in Ogilby's map) stands. It directs you straight forward for Talybont and to the right for Harlech. Either way is full of interest. The way to Talybont (in full use till the lower road was made) goes through the head of Cwm Sylfaen, a valley with an individual charm of bold and simple contours, past the ruin of an ancient inn, and over the Llethr ridge at the Pass of Rhiwgyr. This brings you on to the great plateau that was so full of life in prehistoric times but is so void of it now.

The old track to Harlech also crosses the ridge and reaches the plateau at a point about two miles higher up where it spans the river by a packhorse bridge called *Pont Scethin*, remarkable for its isolation in a wild environment. Three lakes lie near it; the highest, a small wild gem, is right under the rocky escarpment where the Llethr Ridge turns to join the mountain of that name (highest of the range) by a knife-edge. North of these rocks there is a good approach to this summit and, south of them, a convenient way down into Cwm Mynach and the lane which leads back to the main road. That gap can of course be reached by sticking to the high ground of the ridge instead of following the track down to Pont Scethin.

The Migneint and Arennig Region

This is a large and varied mountain group, better described as a region than a range. Its continuity is best illustrated by saying that you can enter it at Pentrefoelas (through which the eastern boundary of the Park passes) and go from thence to Dolgellau, a matter of nearly 30 miles, crossing only two public roads in transit. Taking this walk, with only slight deviations from the straight line, you could cross all the principal summits contained in the region, namely, *Carnedd y Filiast* (2,194 feet), *Arennig Fach* (2,264 feet), *Arennig Fawr* (2,800 feet), *Moel Llyfnant* (2,451 feet), *Y Dduallt* (2,155 feet), and *Rhobell Fawr* (2,408 feet).

'Migneint' is a convenient name for the northern sector of the region as it is marked prominently in capitals on all maps, though it only refers to a small part of it. The word means The Swampy Place. The hill, *Carnedd Iago* (1,765 feet)—The Cairn of James —is the spongy hub which gives rise to streams which radiate like spokes to all points of the compass. Most of them contribute to the Conwy, though the source of that river is over three miles north of James's Cairn on a separate moorland plateau. It springs from Llyn Conwy, famous for its lusty trout and formerly strictly preserved by the Lords of Penrhyn.* Rising between gentle swelling breasts of moorland, with a surface level of 1,488 feet above the sea, its short course thither is fair in every part. In its earlier stage, a little below the head-waters, it is literally gilt-edged in the spring with the lovely globe-flower. There follow the rapids in the defile crossed and recrossed by the Holyhead road, the Conwy Falls, the Fairy Glen, the great salmon pools at the confluences of the Lledr and the Llugwy, the tree-shaded reaches of the Conwy valley, and then that noble estuary.

The country about Llyn Conwy belonged to the Knights of St. John of Jerusalem who had a preceptory at *Ysbyty Ifan*— The Hospital of John—of which the little parish church (rebuilt 1858, but retaining some memorials) is the only reminder. Until the Dissolution of the Monasteries, the whole lordship of Ysbyty was a sanctuary where the king's writ did not run and the rule of the Knights was not strong enough to prevent it becoming a den of thieves who terrorized the whole neighbourhood. One of the broken effigies in the church is of particular interest. It is that of Rhys ap Meredydd who bore Henry Tudor's red dragon standard at the Battle of Bosworth.

On a still more ancient site, at *Penmachno* in the adjoining valley, stands another brand new church. But within, or close by, are no fewer than five early Christian tombstones, four of them inscribed and of unusual interest. One has the sacred Chi-Rho monogram (Plate Vb), another (Plate Va) is to 'a citizen of Venedos' (the early form of Gwynedd), a third mentions that it was set up in the time of the Roman consul Justinus.

Round Llyn Conwy and all over the Migneint, flocks of curlews come in the early spring to found new families. The scent of ling and water plants loading the clear air is set to music by the perpetual trills of their mating addresses. From here you look straight out on to the sturdy forms of the Arennigs, a tender azure or violent purple according to the weather. Less exciting

* And still is, although now a National Trust property.

is the outline of Carnedd y Filiast* and those of its neighbours due east—though geologically related to the Arennig range and the others already named, strung out in a rough crescent to the south. All are volcanic interjections, part of that 'Ring of Fire' mentioned later (page 52). But the country between those milder-looking hills and the Holyhead road has graces of its own which seem to be little explored. The old road made before Telford's time runs through it and leads past Plas Iolyn, a medieval hall, now ruinous, once the home of that Rhys who bore the victorious standard at Bosworth, and later of his grandson, Ellis Prys, the notorious informer, 'Dr Coch', who acquired the properties of the Knights of St. John at Ysbyty. Another branch of the Prys family (the name contracted from ap Rhys) lived at the house a little farther along, called Gilar, whose Jacobean gate-house now sheltering farm implements remains intact (Plate VIIa). These two houses which are so closely related to the history of the neighbourhood lie in Denbighshire just within the eastern boundary of the Park, which now follows the course of a lane leading almost due south to Bala.

The Ffestiniog–Bala road passes between the Lesser and the Greater Arennig. The former lies immediately to the north and, though a member of the 'Ring of Fire', has little allurement. It is shaped like an inverted pie-dish and smoothly clad in heather except on the east side where it breaks rough over a shelf which holds a lake—the only feature which it really has in common with its big brother. *Arennig Fawr* (Plate XVIa), like Snowdon, is an unmistakable individual though not of such finely cut features. It is massive and bull-like, with a broad flat back and only slightly raised head, creating an impression of latent power from whatever angle it is viewed. In spite of its ferocious-looking crags the ascent from either side presents no difficulty to a walker. The more amusing way is from the north end of the lake; this takes you first on to the flat rump of the bull which is a remarkable platform of bare rock almost dead level.

On the summit is an ancient cairn. In 1943 an American Flying Fortress struck the mountain just below it in the mist. Its crew of six were all killed. A tablet, locally carved, carried up the mountain single-handed and placed in position by the bailiff of the estate, tells the story, and the cairn, slightly hollowed out, holds relics of the plane.

Moel Llyfnant is a compact conical hill attached by a high

* An eminence of the mountain shown in the geological map (following page 44) as Gylchedd.

ridge to the south flank of Arennig. It overlooks *Pennant Lliw,* the upper valley from which the Lliw river rushes down to the head of Llyn Tegid through a wild and picturesque declivity, moulded by the ancient fires of Ordovician times and strewn with fragments dislodged by the Age of Ice. Looking up this valley from the main road bridge over the river, you see a striking shape like the Rock of Gibraltar looming up a couple of miles away against the higher and more distant mountain background. It is just the sort of place to picture as the perch for a romantic castle. And if you climb up to the top of that rock you will indeed find the ruin of one—the footings and first courses of a small Norman keep and bailey, all now standing no more than shoulder-height. It is called *Castell Carndochan,* a place to con-jure visions of the olden time! And it will help to gaze on the image of one of the knightly owners of that tower when it was complete, right up to the battlements. You will find the effigy in the little (rebuilt) parish church at *Llanuwchllyn.* It represents Ieuan ap Griffith ap Madoc ap Iorwerth, dressed in the plate armour of the 14th century with three wolves' heads embroidered on his jupon, in token of his ancestor Ririd Flaidd (the Wolf). He died in 1373, having doubtless seen service overseas with the Black Prince. Romantic, too, is the fact that at the foot of that rock there lay a buried treasure in the shape of a gold-bearing reef. Its extraction is a more prosaic story of the 19th century.

The Lliw valley forms a pass into the heart of this part of the mountain region which was followed by the Romans in making the road which linked their fort at Tomen y Mur, near Ffestiniog, with that at the head of Llyn Tegid, within the ramparts of which now stands the farm of *Caer Gai.*

Llyn Tegid has two other alternative names. To the English it is Bala Lake while to the English of former days it was Pimble-mere (Old English *pemmel,* a pebble?). Also the main river flow-ing in has its native name, *Dyfrdwy,* but in flowing out, its English equivalent the *Dee.*

The sources of the Thames, the Severn, and the Wye are all popular objectives for the tourist, but very few seek the far more impressive source of the historic Dee. It is certainly rough going, for there is no regular path and you cannot get within three miles of the place by car. If you follow the river up from the point where it turns into the hills near Garneddwen railway station you see before you, some way off, the wall-like barrier of *Y Dduallt*—the Black Height. It looks like a mountain which, through some primeval cataclysm, has lost one-half of itself and faces you on its riven side. Towards it you mount as you advance, the stream breaking into a series of short falls. Then you come to a wide marsh absolutely level, lying right up to the foot of the Black Height, which rises perpendicular to a crest 600 feet above. This is the source of the Dee which meets salt water below the walls of Chester. The Romans who built their great legionary fortress there (naming it Deva) regarded the river as sacred and should, according to their custom, have built a temple by its highest spring. Perhaps the ruin of it is still there sunk in the peat and moss. But the whole setting is a temple in itself.

From the south end of Y Dduallt there is quite an easy ascent to the top of the cliff from which can be seen the rugged shape of *Rhobell Fawr,* which, like the Glyders, has a double crown (2,408 and 2,313 feet) the last big hill in this group, which has now assumed the shape of the stem end of a pear, on either side of which two deep valleys are converging on Dolgellau round the broad base of the mountain and its foothills.

In a delightful wooded recess between the mountain and those foothills is the village of *Llanfachreth* called after the Celtic missionary Machrith who founded its parish church. The latter has an approach of 19 steps under a lych-gate dedicated to the memory of George III. A road from here leads into the Vale of Ganllwyd and crosses the Mawddach to join the Ffestiniog–Dolgellau road opposite a large National Trust property in which stand the two hotels of Tyn y Groes and Dolmelynllyn Hall (both managed by the Trust) in a finely-timbered park. Near the latter is one of the most shapely waterfalls in Wales. Thomas Gray, the poet, was a connoisseur of waterfalls, and an owner of the estate in the late 18th century linked this *Rhaiadr Du* with Gray's memory by setting up a stone beside the lower pool graven with a verse from his Latin ode to the Deity of the Grande Chartreuse. This is on the fringe of the Rhinog range and two outliers of the same estate are the two sheepwalks (shown on M.) at the foot of Y Llethr, one containing the remote little lake of *Llyn y Bi.*

The remaining corner of the range (the stem end of the pear) is closely associated with the ancient seats of the Vaughans of Nannau and Hengwrt. Here is the long-famous footpath called the *Precipice Walk* which gives admirable prospects of the woodland, torrent and mountain scenery, and in the very pick of it (as is so often the case) is the ruin of the Cistercian Abbey of *Cymer.* It was founded late in the 12th century. On higher ground a little to the north-east, is the mound of a motte castle that can only be a little earlier in date, and must represent the residence of a local magnate who was concerned in the first gift of land to the Abbey. It now carries an 18th-century building made by the Vaughans of Nannau.

Two old bridges cross the converging rivers of Mawddach and Wnion. That over the latter, at Dolgellau, appears to show earlier work. Its seven arches are of three different periods of construction.

THE WESTERN SIDE

The most important antiquity on the western side is the Roman fort at Tomen y Mur, with its little earthwork amphitheatre (actually a cockpit?) adjoining. But the *tomen* (mound) itself is neither Roman nor Welsh. It is a Norman motte castle believed to have been constructed by William Rufus in his campaign against Gruffydd ap Cynan in 1096. A still larger English force assembled here in 1114 in which the kings Henry I and Alexander of Scotland were present with the same object, though they failed to penetrate farther into Wales. At that time the Roman road traversed by these armies must still have been in good shape. The link with Caer Gai (coming direct from Chester) has recently been traced but it is still a question whether there was another leading due south to Pennal. There is an ancient route leading in that direction (part lane, part track) to the east of the road and nearly parallel to it. Where it enters the valley of the River Gain the legend 'Llech Idris' is marked on M. It is a large prehistoric monolith. That it is associated with the same national hero as the mountain (page 40) can only be a guess.

Bedd Porus—the Grave of Porius—was, until recently, marked by an inscribed stone, now carried off to the National Museum at Cardiff. This 5th-6th century Christian is described in his epitaph as 'Homo planus'—a plain man—which has quite a 19th-20th century ring about it.

The Berwyn, Aran and Cader Idris Ranges

The Park boundary takes in the town of Bala and touches the end of the lake. It then follows the road to Llangynog over the Berwyn Hills to the highest point (1,595 feet) which happens to coincide with the ninth milestone. Here also runs the boundary between the shires of Merioneth and Montgomery which keeps the watershed, and the Park boundary turns west to follow it all the way to the sea.

The Berwyn is a delightful range of uniform but never monotonous character. Rising at the edge of the Shropshire plain, it confines the upper Dee to its course all the way to Llyn Tegid. Its smooth, ample flanks are roundly modelled where its many tributary streams descend from the long crest that is hardly lower at any point than 2,000 feet. Its principal heights lie along a short escarpment facing south-east just before the Park can claim them, the chief being *Moel Sych* (2,713 feet). But in those last few miles which do lie within the Park, the characteristics of the range are better seen than elsewhere, as the hills rise directly above the east side of the lake and are open to full view from the road following the opposite bank.

From Llanuwchllyn, at the head of the lake, a road goes up the valley of the Twrch to *Bwlch y Groes*—The Pass of the Cross—whence it descends to Dinas Mawddwy in the Dyfi valley. This pass is on the open mountain, and the name must recall the presence of a medieval cross which stood there to mark the highest point of the journey and the watershed (1,700 feet). From here the mountain barrier continues unbroken, but the road may be said to mark quite definitely the end of the Berwyn range. Looking to your right as you ascend it, a rugged mountain appears at close quarters which is clearly of a different family—another member of the Ring of Fire, Aran Benllyn.

THE ARAN RANGE

Aran Benllyn and *Aran Fawddwy* are the names of the two eminences on this mountain. They are 1½ miles apart but their difference in stature is only a matter of 69 feet. Aran Fawddwy, which reaches 2,970 feet, is the highest of the whole of the long chain reaching from the English Border to the sea which (in this western part of its extent) formed the bastion of Gwynedd, the strongest of the old Welsh states, and it has always been the dividing line between North and South Wales—the river and the estuary of the Dyfi acting as a natural moat.

The names of the heights derive from the two ancient districts of Penllyn and Mawddwy whose former significance has nearly passed out of mind. These two cantrefs* originally belonged to the Middle Kingdom of Powys, one of whose princes was the author of the large castle mound still standing at Bala. He was dispossessed in 1202 by Llewelyn the Great who destroyed the

---

* The *cantref* was a territorial division which could be equated with the English *hundred*. Penllyn—Head of the Lake—refers to the great one, not the small tarn at the foot of the crags.

wooden castle on the mound and annexed Penllyn to his Northern Kingdom of Gwynedd. Mawddwy remained in Powys until the Edwardian conquest, when the shire of Merioneth was created. Its head town, Dinas Mawddwy, then shared honours with Bala and Dolgellau and was made one of the new boroughs.

Approaching the Aran range on the Bala–Dolgellau road, the mountain cuts a fine bold figure beyond the head of the lake, rising from the road with well-rounded slopes and folds to a sharply-figured crest, for the far side is indented with a long series of precipices.

The easy way up is to take the lane at the far end of Llanuwchllyn village where the road turns to go over the bridge. Here you follow the metalled road up to the second cattle grid where you then bear right following a double-rutted track. When you have passed through two gates, bear up to the left towards the saddle between Garth Mawr and Moel Ddu. Here you will reach a wire fence. Turn right and follow the natural line to the top.

Aran Benllyn culminates in a hump of rock startlingly interlaced with veins of white quartz. *Aran Mawddwy* is a steeple-like tor surmounted by a modern cairn and triangulation-point. You may walk along the scalloped edge of the precipice between the two summits (which is not so giddy as appears from below) and gaze over a view extending as far as the Pembrokeshire hills. The last of the Berwyns are well below and, by contrast with these ragged rocks, look well groomed, as though clad in reindeer pelts. At the foot of the crags lie two lakes, *Llyn Lliwbran* and *Llyn Dyfi*; the former sends its trickle of water to the Irish Sea, the other to St. George's Channel—it is the source of the River Dyfi. But perhaps the most striking thing about the mountain is the colouring of the screes which spring from high points in all the hollows and mask the lower face with their trumpet shapes. The rock fragments are bluish in tint and mixed with a clay or mould which supports vegetation. A light green mantle of grass covers them, the blue showing through.

About two miles farther west there is another high point, a dome-like eminence which can hardly be called a mountain in its own right. This is *Glasgwm* (2,557 feet). The map shows a tiny pool at the very top and a small lake in the hollow just below. It looks a fascinating place but I have never managed to get there. The system ends where Cader Idris begins, the division being only slightly marked across a high rolling plateau by the little Clywedog River, followed by the road to Machynlleth which has climbed a hill 2½ miles long from Dolgellau to reach it. At

G

the top, by the four cross-roads, is a famous inn whose sign is the *Cross Foxes* (the arms of the Williams family).

CADER IDRIS

This highly-individual and very impressive mountain is named after a historical person who was killed in battle on the banks of the Severn (presumably against the Saxons) about the year 630. Thus the Park begins and ends with mountains bearing the names of national heroes—the cenotaphs of the princes Llewelyn and David in the north, the Chair of Idris in the south.* Like the Aran, the leading feature of this mountain is its long escarpment. But whereas the Aran faces outwards, with its grandeur confronting only a wilderness of sheep walks, that of Cader Idris looks inwards over the noble Mawddach estuary (Plate XVIIa) towards the populous Barmouth–Dolgellau road, from whence it can be observed to the best possible advantage, its precipices standing clear over a fringe of low wooded hills.

The south side of Cader Idris is remarkable for the deep ravine which suddenly opens at its eastern extremity and continues throughout its whole length (about 12 miles) in a dead straight line as though one of those great giants of the Welsh fairy tale had gashed it with a knife. Its presence is due to a major crack in the earth's crust which affected the whole district between here and the other end of the lake at Bala, after which it is named by geologists the *Bala fault*; the crack is responsible for both that lake and the one under Cader Idris called Talyllyn.

At its western end the mountain is deeply cleft by a flat-bottomed valley which, at its head, is less than 100 feet above sea level. This is another Pennant valley and, like its namesake in the Hebog range, has scenic graces which are quite outstanding, and a village whose old church is also dedicated to St. Michael and therefore bears a name identical with the other— Llanfihangel y Pennant. To the threshold stone of a ruined cottage in this remote village there may be traced the foundation of one of the great world-wide organisations. It was from here, in the year 1800, that Mary Jones, a child of 16, who had for years saved up pennies to buy a Welsh Bible, set forth to walk barefoot to Bala where she had heard one could be obtained from the minister, Thomas Charles. But when she got there she

---

* Idris was a descendant of Meirion, a son of Cunedda, who founded the district of that name, later perpetuated in the shire of Merioneth. It was Cunedda who came down from the Scottish Border in the 5th century with his tribe of Welsh-speaking Celts and settled in North Wales, driving out overseas the Irish-speaking Celts who at that time inhabited the land.

found that the last had been sold. Worse still, no more were to be printed. Charles was so moved by her story and her disappointment that he gave her his own. It was this incident which prompted Charles to make the effort which brought about the foundation of the British and Foreign Bible Society. In their office in London, Mary's Bible is preserved. In her roofless cottage a memorial has now been placed.

The two most striking things in the Pennant valley are the conical rock on which was built one of the few castles in Wales which owed its origin to a Welsh and not an English sovereign, called Castell y Bere. The other is a natural rock, but so fantastic in appearance it looks like a wizard's castle. This is Craig yr Aderyn—the Rock of the Birds. Amongst others which visit it in the springtime is a vast company of the weird and witch-like cormorant. It is surely an exceptional circumstance for these wholly maritime creatures to foregather for nesting six miles from the sea and perhaps indicates an unbroken tradition going back to days when the sea washed the bottom of the crags.

Castell y Bere, whose ruins until lately were largely concealed in the mould of a picturesque oak wood, has always been surrounded by mystery. It is believed to have been built by Llewelyn the Great and again rebuilt by Edward I who went so far as to grant a borough charter to 'Beer', a settlement all trace of which has vanished. Why, anyhow, was this site selected by the great Prince? 'Is it too fanciful,' asks Mr Hemp, 'to see in the ruins of the Castle of Bere the last remains of what his ambition intended to have been the nucleus of the first capital of all Wales?'* Perhaps that estuary which the cormorants seem to remember brought a navigable channel much nearer to the castle in the 13th century. The old church of Llanfihangel was probably founded many centuries before the castle but the Norman font in it may be of that date.

The Pennant valley is mainly watered not by its own small stream, the Cader, but the *Dysynni* river which springs in Talyllyn lake and (contrary to expectation) leaves the long straight valley of the Bala fault to pass into it by a cleft in the southern spur of the mountain. At the point of the river's departure from the Talyllyn valley is the little town of Abergynolwyn whose past history is largely bound up with slate quarrying in the neighbouring hills. This is the upper terminus of the Talyllyn Railway, a narrow-gauge line (2 feet 3 inches), opened for passenger traffic in 1866 and in 1950 condemned to suffer the same

* *The Western Mail*, 22 August 1925.

fate as all the other most attractive light railways in North Wales (Plate XVIIb). It was saved for the tourist by the enterprise of some young enthusiasts who with their own labours put the permanent way and the antique engines and rolling-stock into good working order. In June 1951 the line was reopened under this new management and continues to run during the season. The lower terminus adjoins the main line station at Tywyn.

WALKS UP AND OVER CADER IDRIS

The highest point (2,927 feet) is in an unusual situation where the mountain has almost been cut in two by the excavation of a huge deep hollow on either side leaving only a narrow ridge between on which the mountain refuge hut stands. In each hollow there is a lake, *Llyn Cau* on the south side, *Llyn y Gader* on the north, and the shortest way from Dolgellau is to make for the latter by the well-beaten track called the *Fox's Path*. This branches off the lane leading to Dyffrydan opposite the beginning of the pool called *Llyn Gwernan*. It passes near little *Llyn y Gafr* and it is a pull-up from there to *Llyn y Gader*; but the real tug comes up the next 1,000 feet of steep scree-filled gully.

The old pony route is much easier. This leaves the lane at Dyffrydan and goes through almost the only break in the precipitous face. From there it is about 1½ miles of easy walking to the top.

On the south side of the mountain the most interesting way up, as well as the shortest, is by Llyn Cau—the Shut-in Lake. This aptly describes its most singular feature. As a specimen of what the glacial ice could do it is cited in text books as one of the most perfect cirque-forms in Britain. With its arctic-alpine plant life it is now protected by the Nature Conservancy and forms part of the Cader Idris Nature Reserve.

A short distance from where the road to Talyllyn branches off the main road there is a green iron gate, marked Idris, formerly the drive to a private house. You turn in here and follow the track until you come to the Cader Idris Nature Reserve. You follow the marked track through the reserve until you come to the Cwm. Not far from the lake itself, on the left hand, there is a way up to the crest of the hollow and on round the brim of it to the summit.

The long ridge of the mountain with its formidable eight miles of precipice comes to a sudden end in the west and is rounded off by *Craig Cwm Llwyd* (1,790 feet) where there is a drop of several hundred feet to a wide expanse of grass moor which slopes gently towards the coast. Round this abutment winds an ancient track called Ffordd Ddu—the Black Road. The lane from Dolgellau to Dyffrydan (metalled as far as the mountain gate) is the earlier part of it. It leads to Tywyn or (by striking off it down the Gwril Valley) to *Llwyngwril*. About a hundred yards, on the right-hand side, by the highest point in the track, are the remains of a large round cairn (with a sheep-pen built out of the ruin) called *Bedd y Brenin*—Grave of the King. The Black Road can be reached from Arthog by a branch of it which ascends the steep brow near the waterfalls of the Arthog River. Above *Pant Philyp*, on the left-hand side, is a group of standing stones, a prehistoric site of uncertain nature.

SURROUNDINGS

Bala and Dolgellau. The administrative centre of Merioneth has shifted since the creation of the shire in 1282. Harlech was at first regarded as the county town. Later, the honour was shared equally with Bala, then jointly by Bala and Dolgellau. Now the principal county functions are conducted in Dolgellau. Here the Crown Court is held and it is the headquarters of the Merioneth County Council.

Bala has always been noted for its country fairs and market, formerly held in its broad main street. An old Welsh rhyme gives an indication of the chief source of its wealth. A farmer who has lost his *dafad gorniog*—horned sheep—asks a stranger if he has seen her. He is told 'I saw her at Bala after she had sold her wool, sitting in a chair in front of a big fire, smoking a pipe and calling for a pint of beer.' But the town has not managed to preserve many buildings associated with its long history. Barclay's Bank occupies the house where Thomas Charles, the founder of the British and Foreign Bible Society, lived (Page 40). He has a statue in Tegid Street. The old parish church of Bala was at *Llanycil*, 1½ miles away on the lakeside (an ancient foundation but much restored), until the present one was built in 1855. The *Lake* contains a variety of coarse fish as well as trout and a rare member of the salmon family, the *gwyniad*.

A striking feature of *Dolgellau* is the way in which its houses are built of the local hard igneous rock in large blocks, giving it a thoroughly mountain-made look. Its seven-arch bridge appears to be partly medieval with a variety of later constructions. The parish church, rebuilt in 1719 of dressed shale, has a roof supported on two rows of fir poles, locally grown. It contains the

14th-century effigy of an ancestor of the Vaughans of Nannau. In the shire hall hang portraits of local 19th-century squires.

The Coast. South of the Mawddach estuary, following the fine sweep of sandy beach at Fairbourne, a range of sheer cliffs marks the foot of Cader Idris. Curiously situated on the mountain slope above these cliffs is the old church of *Llangelynnin* (the second foundation of 6th-century Celynin in the Park, page 8)—severely simple with a large porch-bellcote. In it is a bier made with shafts to be borne by mountain ponies. A similar one is in *Llangower* church on the far side of Llyn Tegid. A little farther east, overlooking the entrance to the Pennant valley is *Llanegryn* church which contains a perfect rood-loft and screen richly carved by a local craftsman of about the year 1500.

Between Llanegryn and Tywyn, near the bridge over the Dysynni, is the castle mound, *Domen Dreiniog*, an early seat of the Princes of Gwynedd, before the great work of Castell y Bere, higher up the river, was built; and no doubt royal bounty is reflected in the building of the neighbouring parish church of Tywyn with its arcades and clerestory in the late Norman manner. Since the 5th century Tywyn has been an important centre of the Celtic Church (*clas*) and it possesses two inscribed stones of early date. That within the church is of special interest, as bearing the earliest inscription in Welsh known to exist (c. 7th century).

Aberdyfi, the most southerly point to lie within the Park, is an ancient seaport. It still preserves the building (though much altered) which was its custom house in the early 18th century and was then occupied by that remarkable man, Lewis Morris, who besides being preventive officer of the port was the first to produce reliable charts of the Welsh coast for the Admiralty. He was, in addition, poet, philologist, and antiquary. The time-honoured ferry across the entrance to the Dyfi estuary has fallen into disuse. The iron staging built on the sandbank opposite was to signal from. This short cut brought Aberystwyth within 10 miles of the town, as against 28 by road.

The more westerly Roman road going from North to South Wales crossed the Dyfi near *Pennal* between Aberdyfi and Machynlleth. Cefn Gaer Farm stands on the site of the northwest angle of the fort through which the road passed to Dolgellau and Tomen y Mur. Little of it is to be seen above ground.

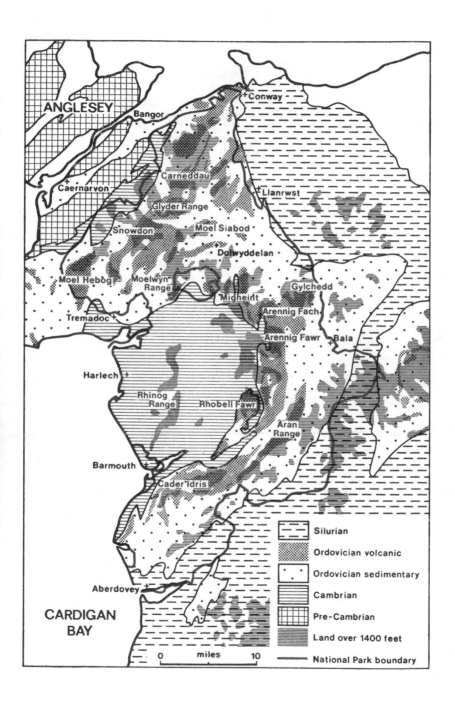

ANGLESEY

Bangor

Conway

Carneddau

Caernarvon

Glyder Range

Llanrwst

Snowdon

Moel Siabod

Dolwyddelan

Moel Hebog

Moelwyn Range

Migneint

Gylchedd

Arennig Fach

Tremadoc

Arennig Fawr

Bala

Harlech

Rhinog Range

Rhobell Fawr

Aran Range

Barmouth

Cader Idris

	Silurian
	Ordovician volcanic
	Ordovician sedimentary
	Cambrian
	Pre-Cambrian
	Land over 1400 feet
	National Park boundary

Aberdovey

CARDIGAN
BAY

0   miles   10

3
The Geology of the Park

T. G. MILLER

GENERAL STRUCTURE

The geological structure of North Wales is exceedingly complex, both in the diversity of its rock-types and also in the way in which these rocks are arranged. Fortunately the strong and rugged surface relief makes it possible to see much of the rock-fabric clearly exposed, and for certain parts of the National Park a great amount of highly-detailed information has been accumulated over the last hundred years—since A. C. Ramsay's *Geological Survey Memoir* was published in 1866.

Although the complete form of the rock-masses is often difficult to make out, a generalised pattern can be recognized, and it is fairly easy to visualise a simple model on which to fix one's position in geological terms. The foundations of such a model lie outside the boundaries of the Park, in the surface rocks of Anglesey and Lleyn, and in two small mainland patches—between Bangor and Caernarvon, and between Bethesda and Penygroes. These are very ancient rocks, of the Pre-Cambrian 'basement complex', that farther to the south-east lie deeply buried, but come again to the surface along the English border beyond the Berwyn range. The two mainland patches—formed, in effect, by two upward ripples in the Pre-Cambrian floor—lie along the north-west edge of the Park, and against them to the south-east lies piled, also in crumpled folds, a great blanket of much newer rocks, that must at one time have stretched continuously across Anglesey and the Irish Sea, but whose worn-down edges now make the main mountain-land of Wales. Within this blanket (itself a series of separate layers) are two huge folds—or one complete fold, having both ridge and complementary trough—crossing the Park with long axes (or centre-lines) running south-west to north-east parallel to the 'grain' of Anglesey (seen in its river lines and the Menai Strait) and the Pre-Cambrian ridges of Bangor and Padarn. These two folds—the trough or *syncline* taking its name from Snowdon, which lies near its centre, and the arch, or dome, an *anticline* centred on the westward hills of Merioneth, and generally called the Harlech dome—dominate

45

and control the position and attitude of the major rock-units of the whole region. The immediate effect is to preserve the youngest rocks of Snowdonia as a filling in the central part of the syncline, and to raise to the surface in the worn-down middle of the Harlech anticline a much older rock sequence. The real size of these structures is very great, for the wave-length of the folds is measured in miles and the amplitude in thousands of feet, while the thickness of distinguishable rock-units varies from several hundreds to several thousands of feet.

Taking the rock-blanket for the moment to be a series of simple layers, the general form of the fold-structure can be made out in a traverse across the Park from north to south. Along the north-western boundary the rocks slant ('dip' to the geologist, in degrees measured from the horizontal) south-east, away from the archean anticline of Llyn Padarn, going down into the centre of the Snowdon syncline, so that, passing to the south, successively higher (i.e. *'younger'*) layers in the sedimentary sequence appear in turn; beyond Snowdon, across the axis of the syncline, the dip-direction is reversed, and the layers come up again in reverse order as we pass outwards from the massif across Nant Gwynant towards Ffestiniog. With the layers (or 'beds') thus now dipping north-westerly we transfer from the southern flank of the Snowdon syncline to the northern flank of the Harlech dome, and the beds begin gradually to turn over, in the Merioneth uplands east of Trawsfynydd, across the top of the arch, until in the foothills of Rhobell Fawr, the Arans and Cader Idris, they dip again to the south-east in the southern flank of the great anticline.

In our model, it is necessary to have not only folds but also *'fractures'* on a very large scale running through the entire region. These fractures, planes of dislocation, or *faults*, sometimes tens of miles long and penetrating thousands of feet into the earth, are additional results of the same forces that folded our pile of rock-blankets—the expression of the passing of a critical point or breaking strain in the whole fabric—causing adjacent slabs of the earth's crust to move relative to one another, either up, down, or sideways. Such movements nearly always produce shattering of the rocks along the plane of shift, and these planes, often cutting across the fold 'grain', may be expressed at the surface as lines of easy drainage or weathering, as ridge-lines or depressions, occasionally suspiciously straight, as in the case of the Talyllyn valley south of Cader Idris, which lies on one of the most important fracture lines of Wales—the Bala fault.

THE ROCKS THEMSELVES

It is comparatively easy to build up a model, but in reality the rocks show enormous variations, in structure, composition, texture and distribution, and one or two of their more fundamental characters must be noticed here, since they control the actual 'look' of the rocks. In a 'normal' assemblage of *sedimentary* rocks—i.e. those formed by the slow accumulation, usually on a sea- or lake-floor, of great sheets of mud, silt, sand, or gravel, now consolidated into mudstone, sandstone, or conglomerate— the most important physical character is the original layering, or bedding, nearly always assumed to have been originally horizontal, so that the dip we now see is a direct indication of tilting or folding. Unfortunately, both these processes—tilting and folding—and the original consolidation of the rock, themselves induce other characters which may tend to obscure or even obliterate the original bedding. The two most important of these secondary structures are *jointing* and *cleavage*, and the effect of these, together with the bedding, usually determines the particular shape and expression of a rock at the surface.

Early in the life-history of a sedimentary rock much rearrangement of its constituent material takes place by means of the simple weight of younger layers accumulating above it—for example, water is driven out of the spaces between sand-grains— and later there develop strong forces that shift the bedding from its original horizontality. Within the rock the effect of these forces is to produce a system of potential cracks, or directions of preferred splitting, as regularly arranged (i.e. roughly parallel) sets of internal plane or slightly curved surfaces. These 'joint planes' usually make high angles with the bedding, and if there are two sets at right angles to each other, and to the bedding, the rock breaks into regular blocks or slabs, and tends to have an 'architectural' appearance. Joints thus frequently control the shape of exposed rock surfaces—slab, gully, or pinnacle, as it may happen.

Cleavage involves a much more severe internal distortion of the rock, and is produced by intense and prolonged external pressure and probably also some heat. These factors produce upon the original assemblage of sand-grains, silt-particles, clay-mineral flakes and needles, or the crystal pieces of a volcanic ash, a gross internal physical deformation—a reorientation—tending to diminish the external stress by turning the flatter or longer particles into planes at right-angles to the direction in which the stress is acting. These new planes, *entirely independent of the original bedding*, become the planes of cleavage, whose closeness of packing depends only on the grain-size of the particles making the rock. When cleavage is imposed on a rock of suitable fine and homogeneous texture—smooth uniform mudstones for example—true *slates* are produced, which will split into familiar thin grey and purple slabs, as in the great Welsh slate belts of Bethesda, Llanberis, Nantlle and Ffestiniog. These rocks will only rarely split along the bedding, and usually the combination of cleavage and jointing makes the whole rock particularly 'rotten' and liable to break into small, flat, parallel-sided pieces, and to form narrow sloping ridges ('house-roof' shapes) and pinnacles, where it is exposed to weathering on high ground.

So far we have mentioned only the sedimentary rocks. In North Wales the succession has been complicated by the introduction of a great series of igneous rocks, and the products of igneous—i.e. volcanic—activity. Most of these are either volcanic lavas, ejected as 'flows' from vents that seem often to have been under the sea; or great sheets of volcanic *ash*, also blown out of vents, sometimes bedded, mixed with mud, and containing fossils; or they may be masses of rock, sometimes sheet-like, sometimes quite irregular, that were *injected* (or *intruded*) as fluids or semifluids into the already formed and consolidated stack of rock-layers. These last, the intrusive igneous rocks, with the volcanic lavas and certain of the ashes, are *crystalline*—made of a more or less tightly interlocking mosaic of individual mineral crystals grown in and from a molten mass: whereas the sedimentary rocks are made of separate mineral grains derived from some pre-existing source, accumulated individually, and usually stratified or bedded.

All this great multi-layered sandwich of variegated rocks, at least five miles thick in the Park area, has been crumpled and compressed into the tortuous fold-and-fracture system we see today, the original or primary structures often modified or obliterated by the imposition of cleavage and jointing, and the fundamentally simple pattern of successive layers distorted by the effects of volcanic explosions and the subsequent injection of streams of molten rock into the whole pile.

GEOLOGICAL HISTORY

We have now outlined the main characters of the rocks that go to setting the shape of the Park's surface features: it remains to consider the present form of the mountain-groups and the dividing valleys and passes—the accumulated results of hundreds of millions of years of earth-history. During this tremendous span of time North Wales has been alternately buried under layers of sedimentary rock and elevated into the zone in which erosion is stronger than deposition. Some time within the last hundred million years it is probable that the drainage pattern was established, not as we see it now in detail, but in its essential basic shape. The latest, and for us the most significant major phase in the historical process, was the establishment, about two million years ago, of a great ice-sheet over Scandinavia, the North Sea, and Scotland, whose marginal lobes penetrated down the depression of the Irish Sea and across the Cheshire plain. At the same time in North Wales small valley glaciers developed, and coalesced into a local sheet with a centre in Merioneth east of the Arennigs. This 'native' Welsh ice-cap was able to push back and deflect the invading stream from the north along the seaward margin of Snowdonia. The great main continental ice was probably six or eight thousand feet thick at its centre over the northern Baltic Sea; the Welsh one cannot have reached much more than a third of this, but the effects of its presence are seen all over the Park, both in valley bottoms and high on the mountain shoulders.

The main effects are two, and complementary: on the one hand the ice-streams scoured off the weathered crust of rock debris that in normal times accumulates on a land surface, exposing the fresh bedrock in deepened valleys and sharply cut-off ridge shoulders; and on the other hand by redistributing all the torn-up and ground-down material round the ice-margin, and by dumping it from the finally melting ice, caused the blanketing and concealing of the bedrock under a new mantle of unconsolidated sand, silt, mud, gravel and peat—what the field geologist calls *drift*.

The gathering-grounds of the Welsh glaciers may be seen today, emptied of their ice, as the upland amphitheatres of the main mountain massifs—the line of cwms along Nant Ffrancon and the north slopes of the Glyders for example. The flow-lines of the glaciers can be seen in many grooved, scratched and polished rock-pavements in valley bottoms and along lower hillslopes; many of the valleys have been over-deepened and now hold lakes like Llyn Peris, Llyn Padarn, or Llyn Ogwen, or have suffered 'unnatural' straightening by the sawing off of projecting hill spurs. Within the mountain groups the debris from the final melting, which took place within the last twenty thousand years, lies piled in moraines—ridges, mounds and sheets of jumbled boulders, gravel, and sand along and across valleys and over the high table-lands, often damming up drainage lines to form lakes —of which the two Marchlyns between Llanberis and Nant Ffrancon are examples.

Round the edges of the mountains the unconsolidated glacial deposits were originally dumped in much greater quantity, and remain now spread over the lowlands and plastered over the foothills in Arvon, through the Caernarvon-Pwllheli-Criccieth gap, and among the isolated hills of Lleyn. The sequence of boulder-filled silts and clays alternating with laminated sands and gravels is exposed in the cliffs of Cardigan Bay. Identification of boulders and pebbles in these beds makes possible the tracing of the flow-lines of the Irish and Scottish ice-stream—pieces of the famous Ailsa Craig microgranite of the Firth of Clyde, granites from Cumberland and Westmorland, blocks of limestone and flint and masses of gravel with sea-shells than can only have come from the floor of the Irish Sea, all these have clearly been torn from their native places and carried far to the south. But the Irish Sea ice never penetrated the 'sanctuary' of North Wales, and within the sanctuary only local rocks are found scattered down the valleys, the stranger-boulders being restricted to the east and west borders.

THE SUCCESSION OF ROCK DYNASTIES

In time following, probably after a long interval, and in space overlying or leaning upon, the old Pre-Cambrian foundation of the Padarn strip, come the various members of the great succession of fossil-bearing strata (there are few Pre-Cambrian fossils), which the geologist for convenience divides into groups labelled with 'dynastic' names in the style of the familiar historical equivalents—Saxon, Norman, Plantagenet—which are used instead of numerical dates to identify events and situations. The rock dynasties of Caernarvonshire and Merioneth, their names appropriately of Welsh origin, are the *Cambrian, Ordovician,* and *Silurian.*

(i) *Cambrian*

The Cambrian rocks occupy two separate areas. The northern is a five-mile-wide strip running, in the Anglesey 'grain', from Clynnog Fawr on the coast across the three Snowdon passes, and fading out in the slopes of Moel Wnion, north-east of Bethesda. The southern area occupies the quadrilateral Harlech–Blaenau Ffestiniog–Dolgellau–Barmouth and is the core of the great Harlech anticline.

The Cambrian of Arvon forms the edge of the Park, skirting the great slate-mining centres of Penrhyn–Bethesda, Llanberis and Nantlle, where smooth even-grained purple and green Cambrian mudstones have been nipped and cleaved between the old Pre-Cambrian ridge rocks and the great mass of the Snowdonian Ordovician to the south. Between Nant Ffrancon and Nant Peris Cambrian strata above the slates stand out as prominent ridges—Elidir Fawr and Fach, and Carnedd y Filiast—built of hard pebbly well-bedded sandstones which continue south-west to the summits of Moel Tryfan, Pen y Cilgwyn, and the heights overlooking Llyn Cwellyn from the west. Occasional bedding surfaces of these rocks show perfect ripple marks—fossilized Cambrian sea-floors; others are covered with sinuous ropy marks and lines of indentations—the casts and burrows of worms, and the tracks of some unknown crawling beasts of the Cambrian sea. But in general there are few fossils to be found in the Cambrian strata.

The Merioneth Cambrian quadrilateral centres physically on the Rhinog mountains—the irregular long north–south ridge running from Moel Penoleu through the Rhinog range and Y Llethr to Llawr Llech, with Moelfre and Y Garn as wings to west and east. All this country west of the Trawsfynydd road is based on much the same kinds of thickly-bedded hard and massive gritstones as we see in Arvon, producing a rather desolate region of stepped terraces bounded by steep lines of crag running up to the main peaks. Round the central grit mass the higher Cambrian beds, shalier and softer, often weathering in rusty colours, underlie much of the moorland that stretches east towards the Arennigs. Here the bare crags are nearly all igneous rocks that have been injected as sheets and tongues into the main sedimentary sequence. Associated with some of them are the gold- and copper-bearing lodes said to have been worked by the Romans at various places in the streams draining to the Mawddach. Gold was still being extracted at the end of the last century, and patient panning will still turn up a flake or two at certain spots.

(ii) *Ordovician*

Above the Cambrian strata, both in the Snowdon passes and on the landward sides of the Harlech dome, comes a great thickness of Ordovician rocks, making a roughly S-shaped outcrop through Snowdonia and southwards by the Moelwyn range and the Migneint to the arc of the Arennig, the Aran, and Cader Idris ranges. The great feature of this region lies in the evidence it provides of a huge outpouring of volcanic material, both as fluid lava-streams and as great blankets of ash, in Ordovician times, nearly 500 million years ago. The solid remnants of these ancient Welsh volcanoes, now stripped to their roots, twisted and distorted out of all likeness to a modern volcanic island-chain, have been called the Ordovician 'Ring of Fire'. Naturally, however much some of the present peaks may look like symmetrical volcanic cones, none of them has ever in this sense been a volcano, and the original structures have long since been flattened and destroyed by erosion.

The massifs of the Glyder range, Snowdon, and the northern fringe of the Hebog range are carved out of the typical Ordovician succession, magnificently displayed along the passes of Nant Ffrancon, Llanberis, Nant Gwynant and Drws y Coed. There are innumerable complications produced by intense local folding and fracturing, superimposed on the main structure, but the general arrangement continues the Anglesey 'grain', of strips lying stretched from south-west to north-east across the valley lines. The base of the sequence—seen, for example, in the screes above Llyn Dwythwch, south of Llanberis—is usually a gritty or pebbly rock containing an abnormal amount of the mineral *tourmaline*, and occasional phosphatized lumps of the curious polyzoan fossil *Bolopora undosa*, but most of the purely sedimentary rocks of the Ordovician are fine-grained, rather soft, dark grey or almost black shales, usually intensely cleaved, and with a peculiar irregular 'rubbly' texture. The peaks of Yr Aran and Y Graigwen are built of these slates, which in some places are so full of the mineral *pyrite* that they carry a coating of rust from its decomposition. The bedding is generally concealed by the cleavage, and consequently any animal remains, which would normally lie along the bedding planes, having settled down on to a flat sea-floor and there been buried by mud or silt, are difficult to see. However, chance is occasionally kind to fossils, and *graptolites*, looking like bits of small hacksaw blade, can be found, for example, near the Snowdon Ranger; and *brachiopods*, somewhat like distorted cockleshells, and *corals*, in the dark brownish-green ashy rock on Snowdon summit.

Throughout this region the main mountain masses are built round the far harder rocks of igneous origin. These include rather finely crystalline lavas often showing peculiar structures produced by their having been ejected on to the sea-floor, or into semi-liquid muds just below it—the 'pillow-structure' so splendidly displayed near the top of the Devil's Kitchen; or through having been sufficiently thick and massive to develop, on cooling, regular joints in three sets inclined at 60 degrees to form hexagonal columns, as on the Lliwedd ridge; or by reason of their original viscosity showing 'flow-banding' or nodule-structure as at Pitt's Head. In other cases the rocks are stratified, and are interrupted not as primary igneous rocks, but as ashy material ejected from the volcanic vents and accumulated in more or less regular beds either on the exposed slopes of the volcanoes themselves, or more usually in the sea-waters surrounding or even covering the vents—all now consolidated into hard massive sheets of various compositions and textures, well displayed, for example, on Lliwedd and Llechog. Occasionally, as in the crags of Cwm Idwal, they contain a good deal of limy or chalky matter, and there is a strong contrast between the rich green ferns and mosses growing on them and the patches of heather and bilberry of the more acid rocks below.

Much of the lower upland at or a little below 2,000 feet east and south of the Snowdon group is based on the relatively soft main sedimentary Ordovician sequence, most of the isolated hills being centred on hard, often irregular, igneous intrusions. Moel Siabod to the north, Cnicht and the Moelwyn range to the south, are of this kind; and the mountains between Tremadog and Beddgelert are a complex of similar igneous injections together with others associated with almost horizontal fracture-planes that convert the whole mass into a jumble of igneous and sedimentary layers, and belts of shattered mixtures. An additional effect, seen particularly in the country round Ffestiniog, is the appearance in the country-rock of a network of hard white quartz veins, which stand out on weathered surfaces, seeming to bind the rock in a tight irregular mesh.

Towards the Arennig range the high ground reverts very largely to the 'Snowdon' structure—fairly regular alternation of bedded volcanic ashes and true lava flows—and this great series, in part at least older than that of Snowdon, carries on the 'Ring of Fire' in a southern arc that reaches the sea at Tywyn, north of Aberdyfi.

The eastern flank and summit of Arennig Fawr, like Snowdon, is formed of a thick bed of ash, with jointing on a rather large scale, producing fantastic shapes on weathering; while the north side, the crags of Maengrygog and Daear Fawr, are of crystalline, occasionally columnar jointed primary igneous rock. On Arennig Fach the stratification is particularly well shown as long terraces on the western and northern crags, where short lens-shaped patches of slate, more easily weathered than the lavas, are inter-spersed among the ashes. The precipitous east side of Moel Llyf-nant, farther south, shows similar terracing in well-bedded fine sandstones full of fossil worm-tracks and castings.

The most southerly sector of the volcanic arc, before it is cut off by the sea, is the east–west range of Cader Idris, whose great bare scarp-face looks north across the Mawddach estuary to the Cambrian rocks in the core of the Harlech anticline. The rock succession is remarkably regular from north to south through the main part of the lower and middle Ordovician, dipping steadily towards the south at about 40 degrees. Only near the summit where softer mudstones appear are any sharp folds developed. Going up by the Fox's Path the first major group of lavas makes the prominent feature between Llyn y Gader and Llyn y Gafr, and the same rocks occupy the whole of the upland valley be-tween Mynydd y Gader and Mynydd Moel. Each separate lava flow tends to have columnar jointing in its middle part, and to become 'pillowy' on its upper surface, often with considerable masses of slate between the pillows. Close above this lava group, along the base of the main scarp, there is a seam of iron ore which has been worked at its continuation near Cross Foxes, towards Dolgellau. The upper group of volcanic rocks begins with a massive ash bed which caps the cliffs of Pen y Gader, above the lake, and the lavas above form the actual summit of Cader Idris and the rough dip-slope running down to Llyn Cau.

South of the main range the ground on both sides of the Talyllyn valley is occupied by a rather featureless series of highly-cleaved mudstones and siltstones. These, with the addition of occasional gritty and limy bands, form all the country round the south and east margins of the Park. Except for the ridge of the Tarrens between the Talyllyn and Dyfi valleys, and around Maesglasau west of Dinas Mawddwy, where there are high-level rocky cwms, these rocks express themselves as comparatively subdued country with rounded hill-forms and thickly-wooded valley-slopes. Into this softer and more domesticated 'rim' de-tached outposts of the Arennig volcanic arc project—Gylchedd and Mynydd Nodol 'standing apart like outraged keystones beyond the centre of the arch'.

(iii) *Silurian*

Little need be said about the small areas of Silurian rocks that fall within the boundaries of the Park. They lie between Betws y Coed and Pentrefoelas on the north-east side, south-east of Bala (above Aber Hirnant), and south of Llanymawddwy on the slopes of Tir Rhiwiog. All these small patches continue the rather monotonous subdued pattern of the upper Ordovician mudstone region that encircles the mountain nuclei, much of it moorland with stretches of peaty ground, part densely afforested, and in relatively few places showing outcrops of solid rock. Whenever they can be seen the rocks are mainly shales or fine-grained sandstones, usually strongly cleaved, and often showing a distinctive stripy lamination in pale grey and green tints. Above Aber Hirnant, on the extreme south-west tip of the Berwyn ridge, these rocks form the synclinal trough (complementary to the Harlech anticline) that bounds the next anticlinal arch to the east, the Berwyn dome, which brings the familiar volcanic Ordovician rocks to the surface again.

THE INTRUSIVE ROCKS

Compared with the structurally similar areas of Ireland and Scotland and the English Lake District, North Wales is deficient in large bodies of intrusive igneous rock—compact masses like those of Wicklow, Shap, or Criffel. Probably the most prominent of the much smaller Welsh examples is the great sheet or 'sill', of granitic composition, that forms the line of cliffs from Cyfrwy to Mynydd Moel in the scarp front of Cader Idris. This sill shows perfectly the development of joint-bounded columns crossing the sheet from top to bottom. It is a geologic oddity that whereas this sill forms such a prominent feature on Cader Idris, another very similar one lower down in the succession forms the broad upland *hollow* between the scarp and the Mawddach estuary.

North of the Vale of Ffestiniog and throughout Snowdonia, thin sheets of injected igneous rock occur among both the soft sedimentary rocks and interleaved with the much harder lavas and ashes. It becomes difficult to distinguish the three kinds of rock—lava, ash, and sill-rock—particularly when their tops or bottoms are concealed. On theoretical grounds the distinctions are straightforward enough—a sill, being injected as a hot fluid, heats and slightly bakes the sandwiching rock above and below; a lava, being an ejected fluid, can only bake the rock below it, and often has slaggy surfaces; an ash bed would not normally have much baking effect at all, and may be stratified. But where the three kinds recur and alternate, and have suffered folding and cleavage and a variety of other secondary alterations, even the most experienced geologist may have to think twice.

H

However, there are certain other intrusions that are comparatively easy to recognize—the granitic rocks (microgranites and 'felsites') of Crib Goch and Crib y Ddisgl on Snowdon; the Bwlch y Cywion granite on the precipitous ridge of Y Llwmllwyd; the riebeckite-microgranite of Mynydd Mawr; the Tanygrisiau granite near Ffestiniog; and many other smaller bodies of rock that were originally driven up as fluids through the main pile of sedimentary and volcanic layers. They are all crystalline, fairly even-textured throughout, never stratified, and usually show a joint-pattern different from that of the enclosing rocks. They are mentioned after the sedimentary 'dynasties' because they are later in time, having been emplaced when the 'host' rocks were already formed and consolidated.

THE GEOLOGICAL TIME-SCALE

The figures shown below as ages in millions of years are approximations: the error involved increases with increasing age but the beginning of the Cambrian period was probably between 500 and 700 million years ago.

Cenozoic periods:	Pleistocene or Glacial	Unconsolidated gravels, sands and clays, often with large boulders ('erratics'), and containing remains of early Man.

1 million years————————————————————————————————————

	Pliocene Miocene Oligocene Eocene Palaeocene	Soft sands and clays, only occasionally cemented as hard rock, with rare bands of limestone confined to south and south-east England.

70 million years———————————————————————————————————

Mesozoic periods:	Cretaceous Jurassic	Yellow and greenish-grey sandstones, grey clays, grey and creamy-yellow limestones, and pure white limestone (chalk). Probably forming part of the Irish Sea floor.
	Triassic	Bright red sandstones and pebble-beds.

225 million years———————————————————————————————————

Palaeozoic periods:	Permian	Red sandstones and purple-red pebbly rocks.
ANGLESEY AND THE MENAI STRAITS	Carboniferous	Dark grey mudstones, coal seams, and yellow or brown sandstones above; grey limestones and black shales below.
	Devonian	Yellow, brown and red sandstones, pebble-beds, siltstones, and shales.

400 million years

	Silurian	Grey, green and pink laminated mudstones, siltstones, and sandstones; black or grey slates.
THE MAIN FOUNDATION ROCKS OF SNOWDONIA NATIONAL PARK	Ordovician	Black or dark grey, rather rubbly shales and slates; pale grey, dark grey or greenish-black, often rusty-weathering, speckled or mottled volcanic rocks.
	Cambrian	Grey, purple and green slates and mudstones, often laminated; grey, very hard sandstones and gritstones, often with dark, massive igneous injections and veins of white quartz.

600 million years

Pre-Cambrian rocks, not subdivided into periods, but in Anglesey and Lleyn probably 1,100–1,500 million years old: Very much contorted mainly grey and green rocks of various sedimentary types including red jasper, with granitic and basaltic injections and black or green mottled volcanic rocks. The 'Mona Complex' of Anglesey and Lleyn, the ridge on which Bangor is built, and the adjoining one south which lies at the foot of the mountains. For comparison, some of the Pre-Cambrian rocks along the north-west coast of Scotland reach back to nearly 3,000 million years.

4

Plant Life

P. W. RICHARDS

There are about 2,000 different kinds of flowering plants in the whole of the British Isles and of these perhaps 900 grow in the Snowdonia National Park, as well as many ferns, mosses and other non-flowering plants. To write a comprehensive guide to the flora of Snowdonia would thus be to write a guide to nearly half the British flora. In a few pages nothing like this is possible; all that can be done is to sketch in barest outline a few of the most important features of the plant life.

At least one plant is found nowhere else in Britain. This is the Mountain Spiderwort (*Lloydia serotina*) (Plate IIa), a delicate lily-like flower which, though very rare, grows on rock ledges in a few of the cwms of Snowdon and the Glyder range. But an abundance of rare or unusual plants is not characteristic of Snowdonia. A very large proportion of the area is rough enclosed or unenclosed hill pasture on which plant life is neither rich nor varied; only a few small moorland flowers break general monotony and these are plants of poor acid soils which can be found in any part of Britain where there are commons or hill grazings offering these conditions. Besides such moorland species most of the other plants which the ordinary country walker thinks of as common, such as Bluebells, Primroses and Foxgloves, are here too, but sometimes in rather odd situations. The bluebell, for instance, which in the home counties is almost exclusively a carpeter of woodlands, grows here in the open; the rough brackeny pastures of Nant Ffrancon and many other valleys are blue with it in early May. The Pink Campion, often a hedgerow plant, grows unexpectedly on the 'hanging gardens' of Cwm Idwal at 2,000 feet and is indeed unusually fine there in size and colouring. Some plants, however, which in most of England and Wales are common, are scarce in Snowdonia or missing altogether, for example, the White Dead Nettle.

A typical scene in the National Park would include grassy hills, open above the 'mountain wall', enclosed pasture below it, precipitous rocky cliffs overhanging the cwms, and, much lower, patches of oakwood surviving from the far more extensive woods which a few centuries ago clothed nearly all the hillsides up to at least 1,000 feet. The plants to be mentioned first should be those which can be seen any day, anywhere in a Snowdonian landscape such as this. Afterwards there must be a few words about the true mountain plants, the 'alpines' which for many plant-lovers are one of the chief attractions of the National Park.

The hill grasslands, whether enclosed or not, are always sheep-grazed and even if the sheep, reckoned as so many to the acre, are very few, they always have a dominating influence on the plant life; it is because of the sheep that plants other than grasses, rushes and sedges tend to be few, and plants which cannot stand continual nibbling become restricted to places which the sheep cannot reach. Thus there are many hundreds of square miles of Welsh hill land which would be dreary enough but for the little blue Milkwort, the four-petalled yellow Tormentil and the tiny whitish flowers of the Heath Bedstraw, which provide some contrast to the prevailing browns and dull greens of the moorland grasses. Among the plants which are soon suppressed by grazing is the Heather (*Calluna vulgaris*); consequently, while in Scotland dark heather-covered hills are a typical feature of the scenery, in Wales there is little heather except on slopes too steep and rocky to be grazed. The only parts of the National Park where heather grows luxuriantly and covers large areas are places like the upper slopes of Cwm Bychan near Harlech, or the few hills which are now, or were formerly, kept as grouse moors. If heather seldom makes a show, the same is not true of Gorse, especially the dwarf, summer-flowering species (*Ulex gallii*) which covers many Welsh hillsides and which the hill farmer regards as one of the more pestilential weeds with which he has to contend.

Wet or boggy places offer more variety of plants than the drier, closely grazed slopes, and in the ill-drained valleys of mountain streams some of the most delightful flowers of the National Park can be found, such as the pale Pink Spotted Orchid (*Orchis ericetorum*), the yellow Bog St. John's Wort (*Hypericum elodes*) with its scarlet-tipped buds, the fairy-like Ivy-leaved Bellflower (*Wahlenbergia hederacea*), the Bog Asphodel and the two insect-eating plants, the Butterwort with its deep purple flowers like violets and rosette of pale yellowish-green leaves, and the Sundew, which has tiny roundish leaves covered with bright red sticky hairs. In more extensive boggy areas on low ground, such as the marshy fields by rivers like the Ogwen and

Glaslyn, an attractive plant is the Bog Myrtle (*Myrica gale*) which looks like a knee-high willow but may be known by its delightfully aromatic leaves and catkins. The latter, which expand in April, are charming to look at but seldom noticed.

Several beautiful plants are particularly fond of the rocky beds of small streams which make their way into gullies down steep hillsides; two which may be mentioned are Golden Saxifrage (*Chrysosplenium oppositifolium*), which flowers in spring and grows in brilliant green masses, and the much less common Starry Saxifrage (*Saxifraga stellaris*) which has tiny pinkish-white flowers like those of the London Pride.

Hill pastures of rough grasses with the other plants just mentioned intermingled, extend to the tops of the highest mountains; even on the summit of Cader Idris and on Snowdon and the Carneddau above 3,000 feet, the flora is much the same except that there are more stones, more moss and more bare ground than lower down. There is, however, a true alpine flora in Snowdonia; it is not found on the highest ridges and summits, but on the rock ledges of the precipitous cwms, especially those which face north and are consequently comparatively little exposed to the drying effects of direct sunshine. It is here that we find two of the saxifrages, the Purple Saxifrage (*Saxifraga oppositifolia*), a dwarf moss-like plant with disproportionately large flowers of a rich purplish red, and the later-flowering pure white Mossy Saxifrage (*Saxifraga hypnoides*). The flowers of the former open in many years as early as the end of February and are much the earliest of the mountain flowers. Among many other plants which like these rock ledges are the Moss Campion (*Silene acaulis*) with its cheerful pink flowers embedded in a huge moss-like cushion and the Rose-root (*Sedum rosea*), a fleshy plant nine inches or more high whose thick brown rootstock when broken smells of roses. One of the handsomest of these 'alpines' is the Globe Flower (*Trollius europaeus*), which is like a large buttercup in which flowers never open, the petals remaining curved into a ball; here and there it grows in the valleys as well as on the mountain ledges. All these plants are found chiefly on rocks which contain some lime, such as the basic volcanic ash of Cader and Snowdon. On the screes below the mountain cliffs the Parsley Fern (*Cryptogramme crispa*) with densely tufted leaves, bright green in summer and russet brown in winter, is highly characteristic.

These 'alpine' plants belong to a group with an interesting history. Botanists speak of them as 'Arctic-alpine' because outside the British Isles their chief homes are the Alps and Arctic regions. With us they grow only on the higher mountains in Wales, northern England, Scotland and Ireland; when and how they got there has long been an interesting problem to plant geographers. It is fairly certain (from the study of fossil seeds, pollen, leaves, etc., in peat, lake muds, etc.) that these arctic-alpine plants were once much more widespread and grew in such far from mountainous districts as East Anglia and the Midlands. That, however, was some thousands of years ago in the early post-glacial period which followed the retreat of the great glaciers of the Ice Age. In later prehistoric times the country became warmer and much of it became covered with forest, but the cwms of Snowdonia remained treeless and continued to provide the cool, moist unshaded conditions such plants need. Thus they are still here today while over most of the country they have long disappeared.

As witnesses of the past as well as for their special beauty these plants have an unusually strong claim to protection. They do not multiply quickly or readily recover from disturbance, and it is much to be hoped that climbers and other visitors to the National Park will learn to recognize and admire them but leave them undisturbed.

Some plants, including the woodland species referred to earlier, habitually grow on the same ledges as the arctic-alpines. One rarity which may be mentioned here is the yellow-flowered Welsh Poppy (*Meconopsis cambrica*); though not a native of either the Arctic or the Alps it grows on the rock ledges inhabited by the arctic-alpines on several mountains of Snowdonia.

The natural woodlands of Snowdonia are mainly Oak (usually Sessile Oak, *Quercus petraea*), though other trees such as Ash, Birch, Wych Elm (*Ulmus glabra*) and Mountain Ash (*Sorbus aucuparia*) are common, not to mention many non-native species such as the Sycamore. Isolated trees, especially Mountain Ash, Ash and Oak, often grow on crags out of reach of sheep and probably testify to the former existence of woodlands at much higher altitudes than at the present day. The natural woodlands have decreased to mere relics and are still diminishing. To an increasing extent they are being cleared to make room for plantations of Larch, Sitka Spruce and other conifers. Though from an economic point of view this may be a gain, the incomparable beauty of the oakwoods still remaining in the valleys would be an irretrievable loss were all of them to be replaced by non-indigenous conifers.

Most of the Snowdonian woods are rather open and the ground under the trees is often overgrown with grass and moorland plants rather than typical woodland undergrowth. The reason for this is mainly sheep or cattle grazing; the woods play an important part in the hill farmer's economy by providing winter shelter. Apart from the usual moorland plants, a flower very characteristic of the oakwoods is the Cow-Wheat (*Melampyrum pratense*) which carpets the ground with gold in late summer.

Damper woods, especially on steep slopes near streams (which are often little grazed) have an altogether richer and more varied flora. A variety of ferns is often found here—Male Fern, Lady Fern, Mountain Buckler and many others; these are a particularly delightful feature of the valleys, especially in spring when the young fronds are unfolding. In gullies on north-facing cliffs, near waterfalls, and in other moist places protected from direct sun, can be found the moss-like filmy ferns (*Hymenophyllum tunbrigense* and *H. wilsonii*) which are among the most interesting of Snowdonian plants.

The Snowdonia National Park does not consist of hills and valleys only. The sand dunes of Mochras and Morfa Harlech have a delightful flora quite different from that found inland and even the muddy and pebbly stretches of coast which are found here and there between Traeth Mawr and the Dyfi estuary are the home of many interesting and attractive plants. The sand-dune plants are at their best in the late spring and early summer when the yellow, blue and particoloured Dune Pansies (*Viola curtisii*) are flowering everywhere; at that season, too, many tiny gem-like flowers are found, minute Forget-me-nots, Cranesbills and many more. Later in the year the swampy hollows or 'slacks' between dunes become the chief attraction because of the abundance of Marsh Orchids, Marsh Helleborine and other beautiful plants, as well as those which are more rare but less striking to the eye. To the lover of plants the coast is by no means the least of the attractions of the Snowdonia National Park.

RESEARCH AND CONSERVATION

The plant life of Snowdonia has been the subject of scientific study ever since its special interest became known through the adventurous journeys of Thomas Johnson, John Ray, Edward Lhwyd and others in the 17th and early 18th centuries. Today such work is carried out actively at the School of Plant Biology at the University College of North Wales, Bangor, the Botany Depart-

PLATE X (*a*) Y Garn from Llyn Ogwen

PLATE X (*b*) Tryfan from Tal y Braich farm

PLATE XI (b) The south aspect of Snowdon seen over Llyn Llydaw

PLATE XI (a) The north aspect of Snowdon seen over Llyn Padarn

PLATE XII (*a*) Llyn Peris and the Llanberis Pass

PLATE XII (*b*) Llyn Nantlle Uchaf, Hebog Range

PLATE XIII (*a*) Llyn Gwynant and Moel Hebog

PLATE XIII (*b*) Moel Siabod and River Llugwy

ment at the University College of Wales, Aberystwyth, and at the Research Station of the Nature Conservancy in Bangor, but knowledge of Snowdonian plants still owes much to visitors from outside Wales.

Like all our native flora the wild plants of Snowdonia are threatened from many directions—by heedless destruction by walkers and climbers, by changes in their habitats caused by afforestation, drainage and modern agricultural methods. Owing to their accessibility and botanical interest Snowdonia, in the narrow sense, and Cader Idris have become favourite places for visiting parties of biology students from schools and universities and are thus important training grounds for the plant scientists of the future. Though this and the great growth of outdoor pursuits of all kinds are to be welcomed, they are not without their dangers for the native plant life and if the flora of Snowdonia is to survive to serve the study and enjoyment of future generations, it is essential that measures should be taken to preserve it.

To promote conservation of plant and animal life the Nature Conservancy has set up a series of National Nature Reserves, of which one of the best known is Cwm Idwal. In such nature reserves access is in most cases freely available to the public, but the collecting of plants is forbidden except by permit and for important scientific purposes. In 1963 the North Wales Naturalists' Trust (Office: 3 Ffordd Gwynedd, Bangor, Caernarvonshire) was set up to promote the conservation of plants and wild life in the six North Wales counties. It owns and manages a number of nature reserves (few at present within the National Park) and as it is an entirely voluntary body, it always welcomes new members.

5

The Fauna of the Park

WILLIAM M. CONDRY

Let us begin with the birds, especially the mountain ones; for the lowland birds of Snowdonia are not much different from those of most other lowlands of Britain. Inevitably the variety of upland birds (and other forms of life) is small. The higher they go into the region of great rains, long frosts and thin soils the harder it is for most birds to survive. Then there is the grassland to contend with. In Britain vast stretches of coarse grassland are always very poor in bird species; and much of upland Snowdonia has just that sort of cover, induced by long centuries of grazing by sheep, cattle, ponies and goats.

But wherever the grassland is broken into by lakes, marshes, streams, crags, heathery terraces, peat hags, boundary walls, old buildings or young conifer plantations then there is an immediate increase in the diversity of birds, for all these habitats have something special to offer in the way of food and shelter. And in Snowdonia there is plenty of such variety. The Ordovician rocks, containing mineral-rich, volcanic materials and spectacularly eroded into peaks and deep valleys, crags and shadowy gorges, offer a wider choice of soil and aspect than you will find, for instance, on the neighbouring moorlands formed on rocks of Silurian age east of the Conwy or south of the Dyfi, moors that stretch to far horizons across smoothly undulating grasslands—marvellous breeding country for Skylarks, Meadow Pipits and very locally Golden Plovers. But not much else.

If you are unfamiliar with upland birds a good one to get to know first is the Raven—nothing easier. Walk the hills any day of the year and sooner or later you will hear the deep resonant *kronk* of ravens and perhaps see their fascinating trick, as they fly past, of twisting over on to their backs, then quickly righting themselves. Ravens also soar a great deal, circling up and up on stiffly-held wings, and that is your best chance of noting that the raven is proportionately longer-winged and longer-necked than the smaller, commoner carrion crow. The raven, very hardy and adaptable, is the supreme mountain bird

64

and quite numerous throughout lowland as well as upland Snowdonia, a typical survival in wild country of a bird long banished by persecution from much of Western Europe including the English lowlands.

Another wide-winged soarer on the upper airs and also long exterminated in much of England is the Buzzard. Though typically more at home in lowland Snowdonia buzzards often float up into the mountain country. And some of them seem to live up there always, nesting on the high crags like ravens and sharing the ravens' diet of beetles, worms and carrion sheep as well as catching many voles.

Raven, Carrion Crow, Buzzard, Kestrel and Peregrine—such are the larger birds of the mountain crags. But these are bad days for peregrines and you are lucky if you see one in a whole week's wandering, so many having died in recent years from eating birds contaminated by poisonous seed-dressings. It is true that the worst of these poisons are no longer in general use and that we should now be able to hope that the peregrine will recover its former numbers. But this will only happen if we make sure that future insecticides are harmless to birds of prey.

Two small birds, Ring Ouzel and Wheatear, also belong to the rocky places of the uplands: not to the summits nor the greatest cliffs but to the lesser crags that have decayed and loosed a great length of scree down their slopes, the sort of ground you find curved like a horseshoe round the heads of many valleys. You can hardly mistake the male ring ouzel's simple song. It is a loudly piped note repeated four or five times, a sound which carries far down the calm and echoing air of a sheltered cwm. The bird himself is less easy to detect. He is not at all conspicuous where he sings, a dark bird perched among dark rocks or heather; and with the wariness of most mountain birds he does not enjoy being watched and quickly slips away into the nearest gully. The wheatear too is fairly shy: but he is easier to observe than the ouzel, being more brightly marked and a conspicuous percher with the habit of throwing himself into the air in frenzied display-flights accompanied by an explosive and scratchy sort of song.

I am nearly forgetting the Wren. But the wren is a bird one easily forgets is a true mountain bird until his startling song, especially loud among rocks, bursts out at you in the silent gully you thought you had to yourself. Wrens you will find fairly common in corrie cliffs up to 2,000 feet, their food the small insects and spiders that live in crevices and under the rocks of boulder scree.

In some places the valleys climb up into far stretches of flattish heather moor as on Berwyn or lose you in a wilderness of heather-covered rocks as on the north end of Rhinog. In either country you may have the luck to see a Merlin arrowing about on long thin wings in pursuit of dragonfly, pipit or fast-flying moth. A superb little falcon, the merlin, but pretty rare in Snowdonia. But the bird that most of all is the bird of the heather is the Grouse and especially so on the wide expanses of Berwyn, perhaps because they are less rain-soaked than moors further west, for the grouse is known to thrive best on the drier moorlands. And where heather country is next to young conifer plantations you should also hear the bubbling of the Blackcock (but go at dawn in spring if you want to see their strange mock battles). This fine big gamebird, characteristic of the moorland fringes, thrives well in the cover of young trees and particularly likes a diet of larch shoots in spring.

If the upland lakes have one special breeding bird it is surely the Common Sandpiper, a frequenter of sparkling waters and stony shores which it enlivens with its cheery calls, songs and displays: an attractive bird to watch, always on the move either picking among the stones or circling out low over the water and back again. It is a stream bird too: right down to sea-level it shares the midstream boulders with grey wagtails and dippers.

Lakes without pebbly shores, where the margins are squelchy and the waters wine-red with peat and half-choked with bottle sedge and horsetails—these are the preferred home not of sandpiper but of Mallard and Teal, the only two ducks that regularly breed in the hills. But neither is a common nester. The upland lakes are mostly too lacking in suitable food, either animal or vegetable, to support many waterfowl. It is true that here and there you may find a numerous colony of Blackheaded Gulls on a lake: but they are there because their nests are safest surrounded by water. Their food they get mostly from elsewhere, flying far to seek it. Big stretches of peat-bog especially near lakes are the likeliest breeding place of the Dunlin but in Snowdonia we are close to the southern limit of this mainly Arctic-nesting little wader and it is rare.

Forestry plantations on the hills are interesting in their early stages. Fence out the sheep and get longer grass, taller whinberries, denser heather. This encourages a great increase, sometimes an explosion, of voles; and along come Short-eared Owls,

Buzzards, Kestrels in considerable numbers. Plant young conifers among the grass and next spring you find them gladly accepted as perches and singing posts by Meadow Pipits, Whinchats and Yellowhammers. And as the little trees reach bush size and spread out to form dense thickets they become nesting places for numerous warblers, Hedge Sparrows, Thrushes and Finches. But the bonanza does not last. After a very few years the bush stage passes into forest that is dark and lacking in undergrowth and is dismally poor in bird life, plant life—nearly all life.

Come out of such a spruce forest in spring down into an oak-wood and the world changes completely. Here among the broad-leaved trees there is sunlight filtering down, colourful flowers are at your feet and there is bird song everywhere; for the oaks are richer in palatable caterpillars—Oak Tortrix, Mottled Umber and Winter Moths are the commonest—than any other tree. This type of woodland is the summer home of a bird that may be commoner in Wales than anywhere else in Britain—the Pied Flycatcher, a little bird with beautifully patterned plumage, very confiding ways, a simple but pleasing song and an irrepressible determination to nest in boxes wherever they are provided.

Other hole-nesters frequent these delectable hillside oakwoods—Tits, Redstarts, Woodpeckers, Nuthatches, Tree-creepers. Here also the Buzzard mainly nests and, especially if a group of larches are growing among the oaks, the Sparrow Hawk breeds there too, for this hawk has not declined in Snowdonia as it has in so much of England.

A brief word on two kinds of sea bird that enter the mountain region. First the Herring Gulls which from an ancient habit of flocking to the hills to moult in late summer have evolved into being scroungers at mountaineers' picnics especially along the tracks up Snowdon. Second the Cormorants which regularly fish in mountain tarns and for at least the past three centuries have nested in a colony high on the great cliffs of Craig yr Aderyn (Bird Rock) four miles from the sea near Tywyn, Merioneth. And there is one bird, the Chough, that you may think of as almost a sea bird so typical is it of sea cliffs in most of its haunts. But in Snowdonia it is mainly a non-coastal bird that especially frequents old slate quarries far inland.

To turn from birds to mammals is like passing from daylight to darkness for so many of our mammals are nocturnal and little known. It is now three centuries since people in Wales could look up from their valleys and see herds of Red Deer grazing the higher slopes. After that the forests became too thinned, the number of cattle and sheep too great for deer of any sort, Red, Roe or Fallow, to have any hope of survival. But deer have spread remarkably in England in recent years so perhaps there is a future for them in Snowdonia. If so, it must be in the greater forestry plantations where already park-escaped fallow deer are slowly spreading.

Predators have fared better. For this is the greatest distinction of Snowdonia—that here still survive those carnivores so mercilessly persecuted (some to the point of extermination) in much of the British lowlands. The Polecat, an animal now hardly known outside Wales, remains common in Snowdonia. The rare and lovely Pine Marten, so elusive that few have ever seen one, still exists in the remoter woods and screes. It is 30 inches long, dark red-brown (the sable of the fur trade) with a yellow or cream chest patch. Another retiring predator, the Otter, recently decreased in much of Britain, is now scarce in Snowdonia also. But you may be lucky enough to see one, or even a family of them, on some quiet lake, stream or estuary. Your chances are better perhaps of hearing them whistling in dusk or darkness for they are more active at night.

Though the keepers of last century managed to finish off the Wild Cat here, Snowdonia is now a region where game-keeping has comparatively little impact. So it is not surprising that Polecats, Badgers, Stoats and Weasels are all pretty common. What is rather astonishing is the continued abundance of the Fox. For in Snowdonia as in all sheep-rearing districts intensive efforts are made by the farmers to keep down the numbers of foxes. Thousands of them are destroyed every year but they show no sign of getting scarce, a fact most farmers explain by telling you that vast numbers of foxes are harboured by the forestry plantations. But what explanation their fathers and grandfathers offered in pre-forestry days I have never discovered.

It is on the multitudes of small rodents and insectivores that the carnivores mainly live though all vary their diet profoundly with the seasons. Field Voles, Bank Voles, Water Voles, Wood Mice, Shrews, Moles, even Hedgehogs—all are taken by the predators. But just what proportion of each prey species does each predator take? How far in fact do all these eaters and eaten extend into the mountain region? On such problems a great deal of patient investigation remains to be accomplished. The Bats of Snowdonia too are another group which have largely gone unstudied. There are probably eight species but little is known of their numbers, distribution and habits.

Reptiles next, a group whose tally is soon told. Two snakes: Adder and Grass Snake; two lizards: Common Lizard and Slow Worm, all warmth-loving valley animals not hankering after a life in chilly, wet uplands. But you may occasionally meet with them along the skirts of the hills: an adder curled in the heather; a grass snake swishing away through waterside vegetation or swimming across ditch or pool; a lizard lying out on sunny wall or bank; a slow worm unexpectedly revealed when you turn over a big flat stone. Even in the valleys the reptiles have to be looked for. The snakes and the slow worm have nocturnal tendencies and the common lizard is only locally common. And all go to sleep in winter.

Frogs, Toads, Newts: all these still flourish abundantly in Snowdonia, though in many parts of Britain they have declined through loss of habitat caused partly by pollution and partly by drainage, especially of the cattle drinking ponds once scattered all over the farming lowlands but now often replaced by piped water. All these creatures are far more adapted to cold and wet than are the reptiles and many a moorland pool has its frogs, toads and palmate newts. But for the crested and smooth newts you will, I think, have to seek in sweeter waters outside the mountain region.

Another group with little taste for acid upland waters are the fish. In any case the Snowdonian rivers and lakes are nearly all cut off by mountain barriers from the more fertile river systems of England with their far greater variety of species. Only the Dee which rises on Dduallt south-west of Llanuwchllyn and soon flows into Llyn Tegid (Bala Lake) links Snowdonia with the English lowlands. So in the upper Dee there are a few fish such as Bullhead, Stone Loach (and Grayling?) which are rare elsewhere in Snowdonia. This means that the only universally common non-migratory species is the Brown Trout, a fish of great beauty which grows to a fair size in waters where the feeding is good and fishing not excessive. But in lakes and streams where fish food is scarce the trout never exceed a few inches no matter how long they live.

In contrast with these fingerlings there are the Salmon and the Sea Trout, migrants which do not trust themselves to our rivers until they have fattened on the rich food of the ocean. (Sea trout in Wales, by the way, are invariably called *sewin*, a word that to the outsider may look good native Welsh. But Welsh etymologists disown it absolutely.) It is towards the end of the year that salmon and sewin, many of which have sum-

mered in lower reaches and estuaries, move far up the rivers to
spawn, those, that is, which have evaded the nets laid for them
in the estuaries and the hooks that wait for them all the way
up the rivers. To reach their ancestral breeding places they battle
against spates and rapids and make spectacular leaps up falls;
and some of them venture so far up shallow moorland streams
there is scarcely sufficient water to cover their backs. And there
they are terribly exposed to the poacher's gaff.

Life is in fact far safer for the two other Snowdonian members
of the trout family, those rare, non-migratory fish: Char and
Gwyniad. The char lives in the Llanberis lakes, Llyn Cwellyn
near Beddgelert and Llyn Bodlyn near Barmouth. It is a little-
known fish living in the depths and venturing into shallow water
only for breeding in late autumn when the males develop a red
flush on the underparts, hence the Welsh name *torgoch* (red
belly). The gwyniad—it has no English name—lives only in Llyn
Tegid and is not found elsewhere in Britain. (It has very close
relatives in the Lake District, Scotland and Ireland.) It takes no
angler's lure and though it can be caught in nets it is seldom
fished for. It is a silvery fish (*gwyniad* literally means 'whiting')
and, like the char, it lives mostly in deep water.

Of the vast number of insect species, I can mention here only
a few butterflies, moths and others likely to come to the attention
of the mountain walker. Of butterflies the most abundant must
be the Small Heath which is continuously on the wing from late
May to September and is usually the only species met with on
high ground apart from Whites, Red Admirals and Painted
Ladies, all of which are passing migrants. Here and there you
might chance upon local colonies of Large Heath, Green Hairstreak, Marsh Fritillary or Small Pearl-bordered Fritillary. But
generally you must come down below the tree-line for the rest
of Snowdonia's butterflies, characteristic among which are
Speckled Wood, Ringlet, Purple Hairstreak, Large Skipper and
Pearl-bordered and Dark-green Fritillaries.

Of upland moths the largest and most easily found are
Emperor, Fox, Northern Eggar and Drinker. Their caterpillars
are even more obvious: the emperor, bright green with rings of
yellow spots; the fox, dark brown often with yellow rings; the
eggar, brown with blackish rings; the drinker, hairy like the last
two but dark grey, a caterpillar much eaten by the moorland
cuckoos. Heather country abounds with smaller moths but they
are sport only for the serious entomologist.

A few other choice insects: the Golden-ringed Dragonfly, of

great size with boldly black and yellow body and common in the hills in summer; the Tiger Beetle, green with gold spots, flying ahead as you disturb it along the track; the Dung Beetle, large, black, violet-bellied, mite-infested, crawling about everywhere with never a thought of concealment though much sought after by kestrels. Many other insects that hatch in the mountain grass are the seasonal food of birds, especially rooks and jackdaws which after the nesting season take their families on daily safaris to the hills to feed especially on click beetles, chafers and the sometimes prodigiously abundant caterpillars of the antler moth.

In trying to find some of the animals and birds of upland Snowdonia you may or may not be successful. Perhaps this hardly matters. What seems more important is the quest itself, a quest that will lead you up into beautiful, often exciting country where you will be far from roads and houses, in places almost as wild as anywhere in Britain. By your searching you may discover nothing new for science but you are pretty sure to do something more important: you will discover something new for yourself that will be, however slightly, a lasting enrichment of your experience. And if you are lucky enough or observant enough to find anything you feel may be of interest to others, or something of value that may be in need of conservation, do please have the kindness to report it to the North Wales Naturalists' Trust.

I

6

Principal Antiquities within the Park

COLIN A. GRESHAM

The boundaries of the Snowdonia National Park were laid out to enclose a tract of mountains and wild upland country, which retains its unspoilt character because it has never attracted human settlement on any great scale. Prehistoric man was excluded from most of the valleys by undrained marshes and impenetrable tree growth, and he only used the highest mountainsides for hunting; thus the districts which he did find attractive for settlement were mostly on the lower slopes facing the sea, where conditions were not too severe and the growth of trees was checked by the wind. This means that the majority of ancient sites are to be found grouped together in those two regions where the Park boundary runs down to the coast, or approaches closely to it—that is to say along the northern coastline from near Bangor to Conwy, and along the shores of Cardigan Bay from the estuary of the Traeth Mawr to that of the Dyfi.

The earliest surviving monuments are the megalithic tombs; their massive burial-chambers, built of huge slabs of stone, are now mostly exposed by the removal of the long cairns, which formerly covered them completely They were erected between 4000 and 2000 B.C. by settlers who came by the Western Sea-ways along St George's Channel, or by overland trade-routes which linked southern Britain with Ireland. Fine examples are to be seen a short distance inland between Harlech and Barmouth and at Maen y Bardd (Plate IVb) and Capel Garmon in the Conwy valley.

Shortly after 2,000 B.C. the discovery and exploitation of copper and tin in the British Isles, and the adoption of bronze (the alloy of these metals) for the manufacture of tools and weapons brought about a revolution in the way of life. At this time also the former burial customs fell into disuse, and from then on the dead were cremated and the ashes placed in round barrows or cairns. This burial custom remained in use for well over a thousand years, and great numbers of cairns can be found in the

72

two coastal districts of the Park, where they cluster thickly on the hillsides inland from Aber to Penmaenmawr, and from Talsarnau to Tywyn. Many have been dug into, revealing the stone cist which formerly protected the pottery vessel containing the ashes, and sometimes additional features such as rings of set stones. Farther inland the cairns are less numerous and generally placed on the tops of the mountains.

The small circles of stones which once formed part of a cairn should not be confused with the larger circles of free-standing stones. These are rare, and the few examples which once stood within the area of the Park have mostly been destroyed. The so-called *Druid's Circle* above Penmaenmawr is the best example, and has nothing to do with the Druids (Plate IVa). Single standing stones are numerous and many of them appear to be set as markers along prehistoric trackways leading over the mountains from ports on the coasts.

At a point in time not long after 500 B.C. the peaceful prosperity of the preceding centuries was disturbed by a time of unrest, probably caused by the introduction of iron from which formidable weapons could be made. The principal remains of this period are the hill-forts built with strong defensive walls of stone and earth. Braich y Dinas on the summit of Penmaenmawr was a very fine and large example, but it has been entirely destroyed by quarrying; there are smaller sites on Conwy Mountain, and at Pen y Gaer five miles to the south, and a number in western Merioneth. The hill-forts probably played an important part in the resistance to the Roman invasion, but after the conquest was complete they mostly went out of use, although some were re-occupied in the Dark Ages.

The Romans held Wales as a military frontier district from A.D. 78 for a little over three centuries; this they accomplished by building a series of forts linked by roads. The fort at *Kanovium* (Caerhun, 4 miles south of Conwy) was on the coast road from Chester to Caernarvon and from it started the principal road to South Wales; this is well known as the *Sarn Helen* (Helen's Causeway), and runs through the centre of the Park linking Caerhun to Bryn y Gefeiliau (a small fort near Capel Curig), Tomen y Mur (one of the best preserved forts in Wales, near Trawsfynydd), Brithdir and Pennal, where it crosses the Afon Dyfi and leaves the Park. On the shores of Llyn Tegid is Caer Gai, another fort on the line of a cross-road running north-east to Chester. The best preserved stretch of Roman road is to be seen at Pen y Stryd, 2½ miles SSW of Trawsfynydd.

At the time of the Roman Occupation the inhabitants of north-west Wales lived in houses substantially built of stone with circular rooms. These hut-circles, or *Cytiau Gwyddelod*, are very numerous in the Park and they are the earliest surviving habitation sites to be seen there. They are numerous along the northern coastal belt, on the Merioneth mountains facing Cardigan Bay, and on the slopes of Moel Hebog and Moel Ddu in Cwm Pennant and Cwm Ystradllyn on the western side of the Park.

Shortly after the withdrawal of the Romans the first Christian missionaries arrived, some coming by the ancient seaways up the west coast, and others along the remains of the Roman roads and earlier trackways over the mountains. The churches which they founded were made of perishable materials and have not survived, but many of the buildings which have taken their places retain dedications to these early founders. From this period in the 6th and 7th centuries A.D. the principal surviving antiquities are the gravestones of which there is an important collection in the church at Penmachno; an example at the farm of Llystyn Gwyn on the western boundary of the Park has the name of the deceased person carved on it in both Latin and Irish, the latter in ogam characters.

There were early religious settlements at Beddgelert and Tywyn, where parts of the existing churches are of 12th- and 13th-century work. Many of the smaller parish churches show work dating from the 13th to the 16th centuries, noteworthy being Llanrhychwyn, Llangelynnin, Llanrwst, Llanfrothen, Llanaber and Dolwyddelan. There is a beautiful rood-screen and loft at Llanegryn. Carved stone effigies of knights belonging to the Welsh school of sculpture may be seen at Llanrwst, Betws y Coed, Llanuwchllyn, Dolgellau and Tywyn.

The earliest castles, built under Norman influence, were earth mounds. There are examples at Aber, Tal y Cafn, Dolbenmaen, Tomen y Mur, Bala, Pennal and two a short distance east of Tywyn. In the 13th century the Welsh Princes began to build stone castles, and these were sited well within the safety of the mountainous district, so there are several good examples to be seen within the Park, the best being Dolbadarn, Dolwyddelan and Castell y Bere (near Tywyn). The great fortresses of Edward I, built to hold down the Welsh after the Conquest of Wales in 1282–3, were strategically placed round the coasts, so only Conwy and Harlech are near the boundaries of the Park, the majority being outside.

The Halls of the local princes of North Wales and the later medieval houses were of timber construction, and have not survived, many of the latter having been replaced by later structures. It was not until the 15th and 16th centuries that the Welsh landowners in the mountainous districts became sufficiently prosperous to build mansions of stone. Cochwillan (near Bethesda) is an early example now used as a barn, and Gwydir is a fine house which is open to the public. Plas Dol y Moch and Glyn Cywarch are still occupied. Important houses built in the 17th century are Parc (near Llanfrothen), Rhiwaedog (Bala) and Pengwern (Ffestiniog). Numerous other mansions, farmhouses and cottages, built during the 17th and 18th centuries, are to be seen almost everywhere within the boundaries of the National Park.

(Most of the important sites of antiquities will be found marked on the one-inch Ordnance Survey maps.)

7

The People and their Language

Although the Snowdonia National Park is largely a rugged and mountainous area yet a community lives and has lived there for centuries. It is a society whose structure has been determined by the same factors which determine all societies, its natural environment, its history and the impact of social forces from outside.

The natural environment of Snowdonia has made it a community of smaller communities which serve a cluster of scattered farmsteads and of small market towns which in turn are the focal points for the villages. The locations of these towns, such as Dolgellau, Caernarvon, Bangor, usually in the lowlands, are centres where the main highways converge. The exception to this is towns such as Blaenau Ffestiniog which grew when the slate industry flourished during the 19th century. And since that period also happened to be a period of religious fervour when numerous Nonconformist chapels were built or enlarged some took their Biblical names from them. So we have Bethel, Bethesda, Nazareth, Caesarea and Carmel.

But this involves understanding the historical roots of the community. In spite of the Edwardian settlement and the building of castles and fortified towns on the periphery of the Snowdonia bastion to maintain English rule, much of the old way of life continued. The Welsh still spoke their own language, developed a literature of superb quality in the Mabinogion and the works of the poets of the 14th and 15th centuries which rank among the highest poetic achievements of Western Europe, and maintained their own laws and customs until the Tudor accession. The Tudors adopted a policy of assimilation which, although it smoothed the way for ambitious Welshmen to proceed to the English Court, was socially disastrous. The result was that the leaders of the native Welsh society became gradually anglicised in speech and habit and between them and the mass of ordinary Welshmen there opened a gulf leading to two separate social classes, different in language, in religion and in politics.

The new leaders gradually emerged from below. The Methodist revival of the 18th century revived the tradition of 17th-century dissent in the few places where it survived. But it became what that had never been, a popular movement. It attracted social sectors never before affected by mass 'enthusiasm'. And above all it created institutions such as the 'seiat' or society meeting where the emotions aroused by revivalist preaching could be disciplined and controlled. A peasantry became articulate. In the following century, as a result of the industrial revolution, this organisation became a political weapon. Dissent became politicised. Its main beneficiary was the Liberal Party in the 19th and the Labour Party in the 20th century.

By today the secularism of the urbanised, industrial society has affected these Nonconformist chapels which stand in their hundreds, stark and empty, in the villages and towns of Wales. Nevertheless they have been of immense importance in the social history of the Welsh community, not merely as transmitters of a religious ideology but as community centres where the young and old could meet to discuss and argue and create a sense of group identity.

The community of the National Park has been affected by all the factors of social change and disruption which influence the whole of our contemporary society. In the Park the population is changing and declining. The two traditional occupations, namely upland farming and quarrying, have been severely affected. In the rural areas there was a decline of some 7,000 people between 1951 and 1961 and this has continued. Since it is the young who emigrate the death rate exceeds the number of births. It is therefore both a declining and an ageing population. Compared with England and the rest of Wales there are fewer people under 24 and more over 60 years of age.

Another factor has been the immigration of retired people into the Park particularly from south-east Lancashire and the Midlands. In 1961 15 per cent of the population of England and Wales were of pensionable age. In the Park the figure is 19 per cent.

There has also been one unforeseen consequence of the cultural history of Wales in this process. The socio-political movements of the 19th century led to a demand for an expansion in educational facilities. The Welsh Intermediate Act of 1889 established a large number of secondary schools in all the small urban centres. Training Colleges were founded in the 1850s. The first University College was opened at Aberystwyth in 1872.

Other colleges followed at Cardiff, Bangor and Swansea. By today there are seven constituent institutions in the University of Wales. So that proportionately a larger number of young Welshmen and women from the rural areas have had higher education than elsewhere in the United Kingdom. But they have had to go elsewhere for employment as teachers, nurses, scientists, technologists, administrators, and a host of other varied occupations.

It is, however, the ubiquitous motor car which has been the most powerful agent of social change. The chapel and the village no longer function as the main foci of social and cultural life. The housewife goes farther afield for her shopping, the young for their entertainment. Many of the men commute to their work in the new factories in the towns on the periphery of the Park. The small village schools are closed. The buses become emptier and run less frequently. And the whole pattern of rural life changes.

The television aerials sprout over the rooftops even in the most isolated farmhouses. Where once the pulpit had been a stage where widely acclaimed preachers discoursed and performed to rapt congregations, other idols now flicker across small screens in the corners of living rooms of cottages and farms. In one sense there has been a widening of horizons but it is questionable whether there has been a deepening of understanding or an increase in acuteness of sensibility.

In some localities in the Park nearly 30 per cent of the properties are used as second homes by people living elsewhere. This is socially a significant development as these people are not a functional part of the local community. They do not really 'belong' to the locality. They are there for weekends in the spring and summer and for long periods of the year their houses are empty. Their children do not go to the village school. They are not part of the societies in which people meet and get to know each other. Nor, of course, do they speak the same language. Furthermore, they can be an economic embarrassment. The demand for these cottages tends to increase their price quite sharply and put them out of reach of the residents who might otherwise purchase them. This also tends to act as a factor which pushes the young out of the countryside in which they were born and bred. Economically these transitory visitors are not very productive. Little local income is derived from them. There is evidence to show that they purchase most of their goods in the supermarkets of the towns and bring them on their periodic

PLATE XIV (*a*) Maentwrog, Vale of Ffestiniog

PLATE XIV (*b*) Llyn Hywel and Rhinog Fach

PLATE XV The Roman Steps, Cwm Bychan, the Rhinog Range

PLATE XVI (*a*) Llyn Celyn and Arennig Fawr

PLATE XVI (*b*) Llyn Tegid, looking towards Aran Benllyn

PLATE XVII (*a*) The Mawddach estuary and foothills of Cader Idris

PLATE XVII (*b*) The Talyllyn Railway, Dolgoch Viaduct

visits. Nevertheless tourism in its various forms does contribute to a significant degree in maintaining the community in the Park. It may be in the form of providing caravan or camping sites, bed and breakfast accommodation, or farm holidays; the sale of farm produce; employment at cafés, hotels and garages; or the supply of recreational facilities such as pony trekking.

The visitor is welcome in the National Park provided he realises that there are people living there whose long ancestral roots create a relationship and induce a passion for the region rather different from that of those who come for recreation as climbers, or fishermen, to sail on the lakes or merely to sit in a coach and stare at the hills and estuaries and waterfalls. It is a vulnerable and sensitive community and resentments can be aroused not merely by the vandals and litter-louts but by an obtuse indifference to the fact that there are certain features of social life which should be respected.

An anonymous writer in *The Times* Literary Supplement on 22 October 1971, reviewing the late Dr Tom Jones' *Whitehall Diary*, comments on his ability to talk to the then Prime Minister, David Lloyd George, 'in the barbarous tongue of Snowdonia'. But the speaking of Welsh is not confined to Snowdonia. If it were, Tom Jones, a native of Rhymney in Monmouthshire, would not have been able to speak it. And although the number of Welsh-speakers has declined in the country as a whole, in the Park over 80 per cent of the people use the language habitually. It is the language of the home. The young child will speak only Welsh until he goes to school. And in some of the remote parts of the Park for all practical purposes the old people can speak only Welsh. Up to the beginning of the century and for some time afterwards the educational policy was to eradicate Welsh as a living language. Children were punished for speaking it in school hours. If caught they had to wear a wooden collar and try to catch another child speaking Welsh and then slip the collar over his head. The last child who wore it was whipped.

Today that policy has been reversed. In the rural areas most children receive their primary education through the medium of Welsh. It is a language in which popular newspapers as well as learned journals are published. Its earliest poems were written in the 6th century. But a contemporary Welsh bookseller would have on his shelves novels, biographies, travel books, short stories, children's books, plays, as well as scholarly works on history, literary criticism, science and politics. It is therefore not a patois spoken only by illiterate peasants, or even as some naive visitors have thought, a dialect of English like Lallans. It is as distinct a language as French or Italian. The appended note on Welsh pronunciation and some of the meanings of the commonest place names may assist the tourist to understand a little better the people who live in the National Park, and to respect a way of life which has survived despite many crises and changes for so long.

NOTE ON THE WELSH LANGUAGE

The Brythons were a Celtic-speaking people who invaded Britain about 500 B.C. They had been preceded by another Celtic-speaking tribe, the Goidels, who settled in Ireland. After the departure of the Roman legions from Britain in the 4th century A.D. the language of the natives was still Brythonic but with a large number of Latin words in its vocabulary. This was an early form of Welsh, and was spoken throughout the country up to the valley of the Clyde. Early Welsh literature celebrates an attack by a force of warriors from Strathclyde on the Saxons encamped on the site of a Roman fort at Catterick in Yorkshire. But in A.D. 500 Cunedda led 'the men of the north' to what is now North Wales before the Welsh were gradually hemmed in by Saxon penetration into Cheshire and Shropshire and along the borders of the south. So the Welsh called themselves Cymry, 'fellow-countrymen'. They were also subject to invasion on the western seaboard from Ireland. Hence some place names are originally Irish. Lleyn is the 'men of Leinster', Din-llaen is 'the fort of the Leinstermen'.

Welsh pronunciation is easier than is usually supposed provided the basic values of the letters are properly learnt. Most of them have the same sounds as in English with the following main variations:

a   – ah
c   – k (hard)
ch – as in *loch*
dd – like th in *the*
e   – eh
f   – v
ff – f
g   – as in *go* (not as in George)
ngh – as in *anguish*
i   – ee
ll – say l, keep tongue in this position and gently blow
o   – oh

th – as in *through*
ıı – the South Walians pronounce as ee and North Walians
    as German ü
w – (1) vowel sound oo cf. cwm, a valley
    (2) consonant as in English
y – (1) as e in the, y, yr, the definite article
    (2) as i in *in* cf. Dyffryn—derffrin

Diphthongs
  ei – ay (as in *way*)
  eu – combine sound of e and u as above
  ai – as y in *my*
  wy – combine oo and ee

Accent
  The accent is on the penultimate vowel, Caernárvon.
  Some place names combine different words so accent on each,
  Pén y Bónt, literally 'the head of the bridge'.

Mutation
  Welsh is an inflected language but the changes are made in
the first consonants not at the end of the word. It mainly affects
words beginning with p, t, c, b, d and g. In place names this
usually takes the following form:
  p – b cf. Llanberis, literally the Church (llan) of Peris.
  t – d cf. Llandudno (Tudno)
  c – g cf. Llangoed (Coed)
  b – f cf. Llanfaglan (Baglan)
  d – dd cf. Llanddaniel (Daniel)
  g – dropped cf. Llanwnda (Gwnda or Gwyndaf).

  Most place names are like the above in naming a Saint or
hermit or add some topographical feature, as in Llanbedr y
Cennin (St. Peter's Church of the leeks) or to denote the locality,
as in Caernarvon – Y Gaer yn Arfon, the Fort in Arfon. The
commonest words in place names are the following:
  Aber – estuary
  Afon – river
  Blaen – (pl. Blaenau) the head(s) of the valley
  Bwlch – pass
  Bryn – hill
  Caer – camp or fort (castrum)
  Craig – rock
  Carn – heap of stones
  Coed – wood
  Cwm – valley
  Dinas – fortified place (now – town or city)

Dyffryn – valley
Glan – bank or shore
Llyn – lake
Maen – rock or large stone
Moel – bare, rounded mountain
Mynydd – mountain
Nant – brook
Pen – head
Pont – bridge
Porth – doorway or harbour
Rhos – moorland
Rhiw – hill
Traeth – beach
Twll – hole or gap
The commonest adjectives (which follow the nouns) are:
Mawr – big
Bach – small
Coch – red
Gwyn – white
Du – black
Melyn – yellow
Glas – blue.

8

The People and their Livelihood

KATHARINE GIBBS

The economy of Snowdonia has from earliest times been tied to the land. At first the area was covered with forest, pierced only here and there as timber was used for fuel, for domestic purposes and smelting, for building and also for all kinds of farm and household implements and utensils. The clearings were grazed initially by goats and cattle.

Gradually the importance of cattle increased and more low-lying land was cleared and drained for hay meadows, and higher scrub and woodland cleared for summer grazings. In the Middle Ages transhumance was practised, a family moving with all their stock to a summer house, or hafod, in the high mountain pastures for the summer months. The household returned to the permanent farmhouse, or hendref, with fattened animals and many cheeses in time for the harvesting of crops grown on the lower ground. In fact, this practice did not die out until after the enclosure movement reached north-west Wales towards the end of the 18th century. In the 16th and 17th centuries the cattle trade grew rapidly to meet the demands of new urban centres in England and annually large herds were driven to markets in Shrewsbury and London.

At the same time the first sheep were arriving on the scene and a cottage spinning and weaving industry developed. Sheep flocks increased at the expense of cattle and further impetus was given to clearing any remaining woodland. In the 18th and 19th centuries boat-building industries developed in some of the ports, such as Conwy, providing another market for timber.

The wool and cloth industries grew in importance after the first woollen mills in the area opened and the sheep flocks continued to grow in size. Most of the Enclosure Acts affecting the National Park area were passed between 1790 and 1815. By this time the mountain grazings were utilised throughout the year, only the younger ewes being brought off the mountain in winter and sent to lower ground. This link with the transhumance of the past remains to the present day, and ewe lambs are still sent 'on tack' for their first winter.

Early attempts to exploit the mineral resources of the region were hampered by poor communications and the difficulty of transporting ore or stone. Slate and stone had been quarried from Roman times onwards mainly to meet local demand, and some lead and copper mines were opened; but from the middle of the 18th century these mineral resources made a greater contribution to the area's economy. The Penrhyn quarries at Bethesda were the first to be systematically exploited under the direction of Richard Pennant, the first Lord Penrhyn. By 1801 a railway had been constructed to transport the slate to Port Penrhyn near Bangor. Soon similar developments were taking place at two other points on the band of Cambrian slate-bearing rocks in Caernarvonshire. The slate from the Dinorwic quarries at Llanberis was exported through Port Dinorwic and the group of quarries in the Nantlle valley used the Slate Quay at Caernarvon. In the Blaenau Ffestiniog district slate was mined as well as quarried. The opening of a light railway from these quarries to Porthmadog enabled the slate to be exported more easily and today visitors can travel on this line and admire the skill of its engineers. A second narrow-gauge railway which was built to carry slate survives in Merioneth, running between Abergynolwyn and Tywyn. In southern Merioneth a further slate and slab-mining district developed, centred on Corris.

The most important area for mining lead and zinc in the National Park was the plateau to the west of the Conwy valley between Trefriw and Betws y Coed. Between 1838 and the start of the First World War up to 19 mines were operating and the output from the best of them exceeded 2,000 tons per annum. The decline of lead mining occurred as discoveries of richer deposits were made in the U.S.A.

Copper ore is found in a belt around Snowdon. Mines at Drws y Coed and Talysarn in the Nantlle valley and the Britannia mine beside Llyn Llydaw were worked into the first decade of this century. Copper has also been mined in a number of places in the Dolgellau mineral belt, which is famous for its gold mines, mostly opened in the 19th century.

Evidence of the activities of former inhabitants of the National Park is there for those who look. The characteristic stone walls separating bottom land from ffridd and ffridd from mountain were built by earlier generations of farmers. Small disused slate quarries can be seen in and adjacent to the Park, e.g. Cwm Ystradllyn, Cwm Eigiau and Abergynolwyn, and nearby are the quarry cottages and smallholdings of the men who worked there.

The hardship endured by men and their families eking out a living in some of the remoter hills and valleys can readily be imagined today as we see how quickly the winters have reduced their farms and cottages to a heap of stones. The economy of the National Park until comparatively recently was based on the rearing of sheep and cattle and dairying, some quarrying and mining, a woollen industry and associated agricultural enterprises. Tourism was already an important source of income and employment in certain places like Betws y Coed. Substantial changes have now taken place—some industries have declined or completely disappeared and new ones have emerged and are growing in importance.

Nevertheless the first occupation which most visitors to the Snowdonia National Park think of is farming and this is still the most important form of land use. The physical constraints of terrain and climate restrict the hill farmer in his choice of farm enterprise and the area is still predominantly devoted to livestock rearing. Welsh mountain sheep are the dominant grazing animals, ranging to the highest peaks in summer to crop the abundant herbage. In the autumn sales five- or six-year-old ewes which have produced three or four lambs in the mountains are sold to lowland farmers where they will be crossed with a larger ram and produce a further two or three lambs in the easier, lusher pastures. At this time the farmer also sells off the wethers for fattening and the surplus ewe lambs, having retained replacements for the drafted ewes in his breeding flock. A smaller proportion of farm income is obtained from the sale of wool. Many farms also keep a herd of Welsh Black cattle, a dual-purpose breed currently favoured as beef animals.

In some of the broader valleys and coastal fringe to the Park more intensive dairy farms are found, but on the majority of farms in the National Park, the proportion of rough grazing or mountain land to enclosed and improved land is very high and best utilised by the hardy sheep.

Mechanisation of many farm practices and the increasing cost of labour has drastically affected farm management and the number of farmers and farm workers. In the 15 years between 1951 and 1966 there has been a 50 per cent decrease in the number of full-time farm workers employed in the National Park. Shearing is mechanised and fewer farmers rely on their own crops of hay and other winter feed, formerly won from the small valley fields. Many of these are now suffering from poor drainage and are reverting to a marshy condition.

The number of farmers has also fallen. The highest and remotest farms are always the first to be abandoned as families move down the hillside to a lower farm and nearer to a hamlet or village. Now that so many rural crafts and trades have also declined, more young people are having to move from their homes to find employment, some on more distant lowland farms and in urban areas. A continuing reduction in the number of farmers suggests an increase in farm size, though there is still a large number of small farms or holdings, some of which must be considered spare-time or part-time farms, as they could not provide a living wage for the occupier. On other small farms, the cash income may be less than the value of the labour supplied, and the occupier would obtain a higher income if he gave up farming and worked for a wage on someone else's farm. However, there should be room in our farming system for people who choose this way of life, forgoing the higher financial rewards of other occupations.

Larger farms are occasionally created by consolidating adjacent properties, but more often by a farmer renting or buying land separate from his own. A typical multiple unit, as they are called, might include one or more upland grazing holdings, a valley farm within the uplands and a lowland holding which can be 10 to 30 miles from the others and possibly outside the National Park.

The hill farmer today makes full use of the stock lorry to gain some measure of independence from the lowlands where he has traditionally wintered his lambs and sold store cattle, wethers and draft ewes. In some of the larger farm businesses, the hill and lowland aspects of the farm are increasingly integrated and this may well be the future pattern of full-time farming in the area. The lowland parts of the unit contain the home farm and provide hay and winter feed, facilities for wintering ewe lambs, lambing for a large flock, enough grass to finish some lambs and beef, dairy and other enterprises. The upland parts of the farm managed perhaps by a son or shepherd, at first living in the old farmhouse but probably later in a nearby village, will provide grazing from April to October when the lowland fields are being rested.

Not all farmland which comes up for sale remains in agriculture. Some may be planted with a relatively new crop—trees. There are now about 50,000 acres of forest in the National Park managed by the Forestry Commission, and 7,000 to 8,000 acres managed by private individuals and organisations. These plantations are mostly of conifers and are less than 50 years old. The remaining woodland consists of about 5,000 acres of very fragmented, mixed, deciduous wood and scrub. The oakwoods are similar to the natural forest which blanketed Wales prior to the clearances for agriculture, and some are now managed as nature reserves.

The first acquisition in the Park area by the Forestry Commission was made in 1919 when some stands of timber in what is now the Gwydyr Forest came under their management. In the 1920s and 30s many forestry workers were recruited from the declining lead mines and some slate quarries. The tradition of the quarrymen also keeping a smallholding was maintained. When the Commission acquired land for planting, the better agricultural land was retained in farming, with a former farmhouse, and offered to Commission employees as a forest holding. These holdings usually consist of 5 to 20 acres of better land around the farmhouse and some rough-grazing rights above the forest.

The openings in the forests formed by these holdings relieve the monotony of large expanses of conifers and are particularly noticeable in Beddgelert, Gwydyr and Coed y Brenin Forests. Today most forestry workers prefer to live in an existing settlement and a number of the houses have been let as holiday cottages.

The success with which non-native trees such as sitka spruce, Douglas fir, western hemlock and lodgepole pine grow here is largely attributed to the similarities of climate found between the western seaboard of North America, where they are native, and western Britain. These trees grow far more quickly than our native hardwoods such as oak and ash, and their softer timber is suited for conversion to pulp for which there is a ready market.

The pulp and chipboard industries can take trees before they reach maturity, so that plantations of spruce and other conifers are likely to be felled at 40 to 60 years. A programme of felling and replanting with a second rotation crop has begun in the 1970s and will increase in scale into the 1980s.

Forestry, like agriculture, has become increasingly mechanised since the Commission began planting in North Wales and this applies particularly to the preparation of ground for planting, felling and extraction of timber. The most labour-intensive period in a forest rotation is the first five years which includes planting and weeding of young trees. Thus, a complete range of different

K

age plantations is necessary if an even demand for labour is to be maintained in the forests of the National Park.

The area of forest will continue to grow but probably more slowly than in the early years of acquisition. The Commission is less interested in small detached parcels of land than in properties coming up for sale adjacent to existing forests.

Agriculture and forestry are the most important occupations of those people who depend directly on the land for their livelihood, so farmers and forest workers make up the major part of the primary rural population of the Park. Exploitation of other natural resources—mineral or rock deposits and water— also provides employment. The National Park boundary was drawn to exclude the main slate-quarrying centres of Caernarvonshire and Merioneth but most of these quarries have now closed or are operating on a very limited scale. However, the large Dinorwic quarries at Llanberis are to house a museum devoted to the slate industry illustrating how slate was won from the hills and exported not only to all parts of Britain but also farther afield. Granite quarries on the northern edge of the Park at Penmaenmawr are an important source of aggregate and roadstone. There is currently renewed interest in the mineral deposits of Merioneth and it remains to be seen whether development will take place.

A number of the many lakes in the National Park are used as reservoirs supplying nearby towns and villages. Llyn Anafon supplying Llanfairfechan, Llyn Elsi—Betws y Coed, Llyn Bodlyn —Barmouth and Llyn Arennig—Bala, are some examples. In addition, water is exported from the Park in the Dee, the only major river flowing east. Llyn Tegid and the newly-created Llyn Celyn are used as regulating reservoirs, retaining water during flood and releasing it gradually into the river so that a constant amount may be abstracted near Chester for public water supply in Liverpool and Cheshire.

Water also plays a very important part in the production of power. The choice of Trawsfynydd as the site of a nuclear power station was determined partly by its need for cooling water and load-bearing rock. Water circulates slowly around the lake, 35 million gallons an hour being taken and returned to the reservoir. A barrage prevents warmed water from the outfall mixing with the main water body until it has cooled to almost the same temperature.

Llyn Stwlan in the Moelwyn range, not far from Trawsfynydd, is the site of the first pumped-storage scheme in Britain. As in a conventional hydro-electric power station, electricity is generated by using the energy of water falling from an elevated reservoir, but in this case, the water is used over and over again. Electricity cannot easily be stored, so surplus power from stations such as Trawsfynydd is used during off-peak periods to pump water from a lower lake at Ffestiniog back up to Llyn Stwlan, 1,000 feet above. When a peak demand has to be met somewhere on the national grid, by releasing water from Stwlan through the turbines in the power station, 360 M.W. can be generated within a minute. In this way it is the capacity to generate which is stored rather than the electricity.

Major engineering works such as the nuclear power station and the dams at Stwlan and Celyn created short-term jobs, many of which were suitable for men being laid off by the slate quarries at Blaenau Ffestiniog at that time. However, these jobs offered no long-term prospects; and though Trawsfynydd employs a large number of people, the skills required are not generally those of a quarryman or construction worker.

What other opportunities for employment are there in the National Park? The most important source is the service industry, manned by members of the secondary rural population whose jobs depend on the existence of the primary occupations. Building contractors, garage mechanics, publicans, shopkeepers, bus drivers, teachers and local government employees are just some of the people whose jobs depend on the presence of others working in the primary industries of agriculture and forestry or in manufacturing, and also on the large numbers of visitors to the Park.

Manufacturing is not currently an important source of employment though works are located at Dolgarrog, Penrhyndeudraeth, Blaenau Ffestiniog and Bala. The creation of small industrial estates in a number of centres in or around the periphery of the National Park is considered one of the few ways of creating new jobs and so enabling more young people to stay in the area.

The importance of the tourist industry has only been hinted at so far. Its development began with the arrival of the railways in the mid-19th century and improvements to roads enabling visitors to come and gaze at the wild scenery of the region and its foreign inhabitants. Since 1945 the motor coach and motor car have given access and individual mobility to thousands more who are attracted to the National Park by its mountains, lakes, moorland, forest and shore. Some of the visitors come for their annual holiday, staying one or two weeks, others touring through

Wales spare three or four days; many more drive out from urban areas for the day or weekend. Tourism brings money into the area as visitors pay for their accommodation in hotels, motels or bed-and-breakfast establishments and also make use of the shops, cafés, garages and visit a castle or art exhibition. However, it is possible to exaggerate the income derived from tourism as the season is fairly short and many visitors choose relatively inexpensive types of accommodation such as camping or caravanning. Self-catering holidays are common and it is noticeable that many people bring groceries to last their stay from urban supermarkets, buying only petrol and the odd ice-cream, packet of cigarettes and pint of beer in the National Park.

On the other hand, much is now provided for the visitor to help him enjoy his stay. There are increasing numbers of well-sited, free car parks and lay-bys; 14 picnic sites provided by the Forestry Commission and a network of public footpaths. For the price of a leaflet you can enjoy a variety of mountain, farm, forest and nature trails managed by the Nature Conservancy, the Information Service of the Snowdonia Park Joint Advisory Committee or the Forestry Commission. Should we expect to get so much for so little expense to ourselves? Does the landowner get any recompense for having numbers of people disporting themselves on his land?

Usually not directly, but an increasing number of farmers are benefiting by adding a recreation enterprise to their more orthodox farming activities. The choice depends on the location of the farm and the aptitude of the farmer and his wife. Maintaining a small camping site, selling produce at the farm gate and using a spare bedroom for bed-and-breakfast trade are the commonest activities. However important tourism becomes to the economy of the Snowdonia National Park, increasing the dependence of the area on service industries, we must hope that the sheep will not be driven from the mountains because there are no longer enough men in the valleys to gather them or the return for their labours is too small. For the hill farmer is an integral part of the life of the Park, both to the communities living within its boundaries and to the visitors who come to share its splendours.

9

Recreation in the Snowdonia National Park

JOHN GITTINS

During the latter part of the 19th century the railways opened up North Wales to a minority but it has been the internal combustion engine which has spear-headed universal participation in recreation within what is now the Snowdonia National Park.

Yet even in the 1970s, with increasing visitor use, we can still find solitude with the aid of the relevant maps and an ability to use them. Nevertheless the findings of research work in Britain, Holland and the United States of America reveal that most of us don't in the least want to get away from other people; on the contrary crowds mean 'we've come to the right place'.

The National Park can be divided into three zones:
1 miles of coastline;
2 a lowland agricultural belt; and
3 the uplands—land over 800 feet.

It is these physical resources, which include forests, lakes and rivers, that make up the landscape. Man and his animals play an important role and climate, rock structure and vegetation combine to make the area one of great natural beauty.

In recent years the claims of recreation as a land-using activity have been increasingly acknowledged. In upland areas where most of the agricultural production depends on the use of semi-natural grassland with little or no cropping, recreation use can be complementary to farming, although at very high levels of recreational intensity the two may become competitive. Apart from the early stages when forests are being established, recreation and forestry are in most instances complementary. The extensive nature of most activities is particularly important and access a key factor in the enjoyment of the recreation experience. While the use of water resources often requires special attention, the integration of recreation with other land uses is possible.

Walking. Snowdonia, due to its geological structure and topography, is one of the most popular walking areas in Britain. Deep cwms, steep cliffs and long ridges lead to summits from

which exceptionally fine views of the surrounding mountains,
lakes, sea and forest can be enjoyed. Mountain masses like the
Carneddau and the Rhinog range offer a challenge to the keen
rambler similar to that of the Highlands of Scotland. Areas
such as the Gwydyr, Beddgelert, Coed y Brenin and Dyfi
Forests; the Cregennen Lakes and the north side of the Mawddach estuary provide facilities for walkers who do not wish to
visit the high mountains, but nevertheless want to enjoy fine
views, undulating terrain, open moorlands, trees, sheets of water
and evidence of past industrial use.

The main routes vary from those to the top of the fourteen
challenging 3,000 ft. peaks of North Snowdonia, a large section
of the 'Cambrian Way' and the Snowdon Horseshoe, to individual summits and low-level walks. Yr Wyddfa (3,560 ft.), the
highest peak in England and Wales, is the most popular mountain
in the Park, with six principal walking routes to the summit,
plus a rack and pinion railway. Tryfan and the Glyders, the
Carneddau, Cnicht and Moel Siabod in the northern section are
popular, while Cader Idris, the Aran, and to a lesser extent, the
Arennig and Rhinog ranges in the south attract keen walkers.

Rock Climbing. North Snowdonia is a centre of rock climbing
in Britain. Since the pioneering days of local men like J. M. Archer
Thompson and his friends; O. G. Jones; the Abrahams brothers;
A. W. Andrews; 'Steeple' Barlow and later G. Winthrop Young
with his Easter parties of pre-Great War days, the crags have
been climbed by succeeding generations of rock climbers.

Geologically most of the crags used for climbing are igneous
rocks of Ordovician age. This probably accounts for the con-
sistent character of climbing in the area. Most of the crags are
relatively small and steep. The rock itself is usually clean and
sound. Owing to the distribution of geological and geomorphological features, most of the crags used by rock climbers are
situated in the Caernarvonshire section of the Park, where tradition and easy access from the roadside has led to their development. Nevertheless, some particularly fine crags are located
away from the road network. For example, Ysgoliau Duon and
Craig yr Ysfa on the Carneddau, Clogwyn Du'r Arddu in the
Snowdon Massif and Cwm Silyn are also popular climbing areas.

Today, over 1,500 recognized climbing routes exist on crags
throughout the Park, and additional climbs or variations are
added annually. Most of the routes in the area are in the region
of 75 feet to 200 feet in height, although by linking routes, climbs
of 800 feet can be obtained on cliffs such as Lliwedd. The routes

on crags in the area offer full scope for climbers to use the various techniques available to ascend buttresses, slabs, walls, gullies, corners, chimneys and cracks.

Rock climbing routes are graded by experienced climbers who compile or revise guide-books to particular areas, based on a recognized scale of seven standards from 'Easy' to 'Exceptionally Severe'. Guide-books issued by the "Climbers' Club" give details of the routes grouped into areas or particular mountains.

Each winter more mountaineers visit Snowdonia to climb on snow and ice. Under suitable conditions, a wide range of opportunities are available. These vary from mountaineering expeditions like the Snowdon Horseshoe and the Glyder range to gully climbing on Clogwyn y Garnedd (Snowdon) and the alpine-like cliffs of Lliwedd and Ysgoliau Duon on the Carneddau.

In Snowdonia, it is possible most years to climb on snow and ice from mid-December until the end of April. To date, 1972, it is estimated that about 45 per cent of the possible snow and ice routes in the Park have been climbed. Most of the best cliffs face north or east, where they obtain little direct sunlight and the snow and ice remain for long periods. The main routes are on crags and gullies above 2,000 feet, allowing for an average of 500 feet of climbing.

Ski-ing. In recent years there has been an upsurge in the number of people ski-ing. It is possible for keen devotees to ski albeit intermittently between January and March. There are three possible ways of obtaining a suitable surface for ski-ing:

1 Natural snow—particularly on the Carneddau and Migneint Moors south-west of Ysbyty Ifan.
2 Machine-made snow—produced by a device working on the same principle as a lawn-sprayer. A fine spray of water is ejected under pressure and freezes into snow crystals as it falls. The method is effective within three degrees of freezing point (35 degs. F.) and below.
3 Nylon slopes—these consist of composition brush matting acting as a substitute surface. A downhill slope is in use at the National Mountaineering Centre, Capel Curig. In woods nearby, on undulating terrain, there is also a cross-country run.

It is therefore possible to ski in the Park. On Foel Grach in the Carneddau upwards of three months' ski-ing is often available but the terrain makes access difficult. The runs, which average 250 yards, are on grassy slopes at between 2,500 and 3,000 feet. Elsewhere the length of the 'season' depends on snowfall; only in exceptional years does this provide more than six weeks' ski-ing. While it would be short-sighted to completely write off future ski-ing development there is at present a lack of information about the number of days in each year with snow lying on the ground, the extent of the snow area, and information relating to snow depth both on exposed slopes and in drifted hollows. There is possibly some scope for small-scale projects which might include the use of inexpensive but effective fencing to channel snow into gullies, thereby increasing the length of ski-runs and ski-days, together with the provision of portable ski-tows to facilitate access in the immediate area of the slopes.

Orienteering. Orienteering originated in Scandinavia. The sport, which resembles a cross-country race using a map and compass, can take the form of a race between individuals, teams or relay teams. The competitors pass through control points whose locations are indicated by grid references marked either on a master map at the start or given at the preceding control. Between central points, individual runners plan their own routes dependent on personal judgement. In most competitions, competitors start at intervals. As a recreational activity and an educational pursuit, the sport has its value in that it develops great accuracy in map reading and compass work; skill in way finding being in many instances as valuable a quality in a race as sheer speed and endurance.

The forest areas of Gwydyr, Coed y Brenin and Dyfi with their undulating landscape, well-wooded slopes and dense undergrowth in places, provide superb locations for training and competition. Upland farm areas should be avoided. Since 1965 the 'Welsh Championship' has been held at Capel Curig, attracting entries from England, Scotland and Wales. In 1971 an international event was held at Capel Curig.

Orienteering is an all-year, all-weather sport, with day and night events. Most outdoor education centres in the Park include orienteering in their programmes. The Park has some of the best terrain for this activity in Britain, and is near to the conurbations of Merseyside and the Midlands, where the sport is strong. The future of the sport looks very bright with growing numbers of participants and events. Because the sport and individual events are well organised, it is unlikely that conflict will arise with either other recreationists or the Forestry Commission on whose land most events are held.

Pony Trekking. Although the terrain is suitable, pony trekking is not a common pursuit in the Park. Scope exists for further development in many parts of the area, particularly in the Gwydyr Plateau above Llanrwst and Betws y Coed. Past experience suggests that there is little conflict between the activity and other recreational pursuits or land-using activities. Care is needed, however, when planning routes to avoid areas where heavy use could result in erosion.

Fishing. Abundant facilities for fishing are to be found in the National Park. These include rivers, streams, lakes and the sea coast. Game fishing predominates with salmon, migratory trout and brown trout being the quarry. In the Llanberis Lakes, Padarn and Peris, a rare char, the 'torgoch', is taken; in Llyn Tegid, the 'gwyniad' can, with luck and skill, be caught. There is some coarse fishing available, for instance, pike in Llyn Tegid.

Licences issued by the two river authorities whose jurisdiction covers the Park—the Gwynedd or the Dee and Clwyd River Authorities—are necessary to fish inland waters in the Park.

There are six ways by which visitors to the Park can undertake fishing as an activity:

1 By purchasing a stretch of river or lake;
2 Some hotels and caravan parks either own or lease fishing rights, or have arrangements with local associations by which visitors can obtain permits. A few hotels offer an 'all inclusive' fishing tariff, with a choice of fishing;
3 Some local Angling Associations issue day or weekly permits through local secretaries, village shops and garages. Public authorities, notably the C.E.G.B. and Joint Water Boards, sell permits for lake fishing. A few private landlords and estates also sell visitor permits;
4 By obtaining membership of one of the English Angling Associations which own or lease fisheries in the Park;
5 By purchasing a River Authority Licence and fishing on stretches of 'free' fishing, for example, the River Dysynni's *north bank* from the old boat-house to the sea;
6 By purchasing a River Authority licence and a season, week or day permit to fish waters owned by bodies such as the Forestry Commission and National Trust.

Without a doubt the successful provision and subsequent maintenance of facilities for fishing both in rivers and lakes depends on a careful management programme. Both river authorities pay particular attention to the three main aspects of management which are directly related to fishing, namely improving the river bed; fish rearing and re-stocking programmes; and research, both fundamental and applied.

The coastal waters around the Park, including the many estuaries, provide sea fishing facilities which range from average to excellent. Because no licence is required for sea fishing, the activity is particularly attractive to both residents and visitors.

There are three main approaches to sea fishing:

(a) *Beach*—particularly along the North Caernarvonshire coast. The Menai Straits, although not in the Park, is a popular area as is the Dysynni estuary;

(b) *Piers*—offer good vantage points for sea fishing. Penmaenmawr, Barmouth Bridge and Bangor are used by both local and visiting fishermen;

(c) *Boats*—fishing from boats is popular throughout the area. The main fish caught are Bass, Tope, Pollock, Skate, Mullet, Plaice, and Mackerel, with Cod and Whiting in winter.

Canoeing. There are many rivers, lakes, estuaries and stretches of sea coast suitable for canoeing. At the present time six lakes, four rivers (whole or part) and four estuaries are used for this purpose. Sea canoeing is practised at various points along the Caernarvonshire and Merioneth sea coast, with canoe surfing at Harlech and at Black Rock Sands, Porthmadog, just outside the Park boundary.

Sailing. Coastal and inland waters in or near the Park are popular sailing locations. The Countryside Commission in their recent report on the North Wales Coast stressed that coastal areas were experiencing the effect of a national boom in sailing.

The most popular coastal waters include the North Caernarvonshire coast, from Caernarvon to Deganwy, and the Merioneth sea coast (all of which, with the exception of nine miles, is in the Park). Llyn Tegid is by far the most popular inland water. Use is also made of Llyn Geirionydd.

There are 12 sailing clubs situated in or near the Park. Between 1960 and 1966 there was a 77 per cent increase in sailing club membership in Caernarvonshire, while club sailing accounted for over 40 per cent of all craft sailing around the North Wales coast. Although club sailing predominates throughout the area, sailing by 'non-club' participants also takes place from beaches throughout the area or from the lakeside of Llyn Tegid. Visitors to the area can also use man-made facilities provided by clubs in a number of locations.

The location of the most popular sailing areas, sailing clubs and dinghy parks coincide. In 1966 there was mooring space for 5,200 boats in dinghy parks along the coast, 70 per cent of which are in Caernarvonshire at Abersoch, Conwy, Port Dinorwic, Porthmadog and Pwllheli.

Power Boating and Water Ski-ing. Power boating and water ski-ing have been activities at the centre of considerable debate. The noise factor is a critical aspect whilst the possible danger— essentially physical in nature—to other water users is important. Professor Allen, consultant to the Snowdonia Park Joint Advisory Committee, reporting on the future recreation value of Llynnau Tegid and Celyn said 'whilst it is tempting to find more opportunities for this increasingly popular sport, it is not in my view appropriate in this part of the National Park'.

In 1971 five locations in or near the Snowdonia National Park were being used for power boating and water ski-ing, Llyn Geirionydd, sections of the Mawddach estuary, the sea at Barmouth, Morfa Harlech and Penmaenmawr. There is wide variation in the intensity of use, Llyn Geirionydd and the Barmouth/Mawddach estuary being the most popular locations.

Beaches. The seaside is particularly popular with visitors; overall it is probably the most popular recreation resource in North Wales. There are fine beaches on the Caernarvonshire coast at Conwy, Penmaenmawr, Llanfairfechan, Morfa Bychan and Porthmadog, and on the Cardigan Bay coast at Harlech, Llanbedr, Llanenddwyn, Talybont, Llanaber, Fairbourne, Tywyn and Aberdyfi. Swimming, sun bathing and children's or beach games are the most popular activities; in addition beaches are used by fishermen, canoeists, sailors, water skiers and naturalists.

Beach access is normally free, except for car parking or access to controlled beaches such as Shell Island, Mochras and Black Rock Sands. Along many parts of the coast, the narrow twisting roads in spite of peak period congestion form an integral part of the landscape character of the area, and as such should not —save in a few cases—be widened.

Some lakes and rivers are used for swimming; Llyn Tegid being particularly popular, and is the venue for many long-distance swimming championships.

Motor Sport. No account of use made for recreation of resources in the Park would be complete without mention of areas in the Park used for organised motor sport. Motor car rallying and motor cycle scrambling are the main types of use.

These activities are strictly controlled by legal requirements. Forestry Commission land in Dyfi, Coed y Brenin, and Gwydyr Forests is used for special stages. Without the use of these forest roads, for which payment is made, it would be impossible to hold rallies in Britain. About 12 rallies are held annually, using part of the Park, four of which are of international or national standing. Large crowds are attracted to the major events, for example an estimated crowd of 5,000 saw the Gwydyr Forest stages of the Royal Automobile Club's International Rally in 1968.

Motor cycle scrambling, organised under the auspices of the Auto-Cycle Union, is held near Bala on terrain which offers many excellent vantage points for spectators. These events take place on private farmland and are organised by local clubs.

This is the picture of recreation use in terms of landscape resources in the Park. Most of the activities take place in the Park because the area offers facilities which cannot be bettered elsewhere in Britain.

NATURAL HISTORY AS A RECREATIONAL ACTIVITY

The large areas of mountain grassland of different types, moorland, upland lakes and streams, the scrub woodland and forests are habitats for many interesting forms of wild life. This diversity of landscape and the associated animal and plant life is a base for recreation and education.

Botanically the area has been famous since the 17th century. Geology as a science was born in Snowdonia. The herds of feral goats found on Snowdon, Cwm Idwal, Rhinog and Cader Idris are examples of animals close to the northern limits of their range. The Chough—a red-beaked, red-legged member of the Crow family—the Dipper, Buzzard and Ring Ouzel also attract attention.

Indeed, specialist geologists, ornithologists, botanists or interested laymen, armed with cameras, binoculars and field guidebooks, are coming to Snowdonia in ever-increasing numbers. Evidence suggests natural history, father of the 'new' science—ecology, will grow as a recreational activity.

THE IMPACT OF VISITORS

Visitor impact is mainly connected with peak period use. Road traffic congestion is a perennial feature of recreation in the Park. Problems connected with visitor impact on land and water resources fall under three headings: erosion, trespass and litter. Some beaches and many of the main paths to mountain summits are showing signs of erosion through intensive use.

In some areas trespass (or access), depending on which side of the fence one is placed, is a problem. Most damage is caused at or near the roadside. Apart from picnicking in hayfields, damaging walls and other types of field boundary, this problem of damage by visitors is related to the demands made by visitors wishing to cross the 'bottom' land in order to walk to mountain summits.

Litter is a major problem particularly during the peak summer months and although steps are taken to educate the British public to follow all ten rules of the 'Country Code' it will be many years, if at all, before we get majority backing. As H.M. the Queen Mother said to Sir Clough Williams-Ellis in 1943 when he outlined his vision of a national park in Snowdonia, standing at the Penygwryd cross-roads—'It's fine your preparing this splendid countryside for the people, but are you doing anything about preparing the people to make proper use of it?'

One may well ask what has been done? Since its inception the Snowdonia Park Joint Advisory Committee have opened six permanent information centres and one mobile in the Park. They are the first National Park body to purchase a building intended as a residential centre providing visitors with increased knowledge of the life and landscape.

Crystal-ball gazing can be fun, it can also be dangerous. However, my view from the ball in 1972 shows a future which will bring more visitors, many of whom will engage in active recreation pursuits in a Park which is national in the sense that it is recognized as an area of exceptional national value where existing land uses can go hand in hand with recreation usage. Indeed, with the continuing growth of world-wide tourism I see the Snowdonia National Park—Parc Cenedlaethol Eryri—as a park of international standing.

BIBLIOGRAPHY

GENERAL

CAERNARVONSHIRE COUNTY COUNCIL. *Caernarvonshire: the County Handbook.* 1969.

CARR, H. R. C. and LISTER, G. A. (eds.) *The Mountains of Snowdonia.* 1948. Crosby Lockwood.

CONDRY, W. M. *The Snowdonia National Park.* (New Naturalist Series) 1966. Collins.

DAVIES, E. and REES, A. D. (eds.) *Welsh Rural Communities.* 1962. University of Wales Press.

DAVIES, M. *National Parks of Wales.* 1970. Cardiff Naturalists' Association.

EMMETT, I. *A North Wales Village: a social anthropological study.* 1964. Routledge and Kegan Paul.

LOVINS, A. and EVANS, P. *Eryri, the Mountains of Longing.* 1972. Friends of the Earth/George Allen and Unwin Ltd.

MERIONETH COUNTY COUNCIL. *Merioneth County Handbook.* 1972.

NORTH, F. J., CAMPBELL, B., SCOTT, R. *Snowdonia: the National Park of North Wales.* (New Naturalist Series) 1949. Collins.

ARCHAEOLOGY AND HISTORY

DODD, A. H. *The Industrial Revolution in North Wales.* 2nd ed. 1951. University of Wales Press.

NASH-WILLIAMS, V. E. *The Roman Frontier in Wales.* 1969. University of Wales Press.

PEATE, I. C. *The Welsh House.* 1946. Hugh Evans and Sons Ltd., Liverpool.

WATSON, K. *North Wales.* 1967. Heinemann Regional Archaeologies.

Caernarvonshire: a survey and inventory by the Royal Commission on the Ancient and Historical Monuments in Wales and Monmouthshire. Vol. 1: East, 1956. Vol. 2: Central, 1960. HMSO.

FORESTRY

FORESTRY COMMISSION. *The Cambrian Forests.* 1959. HMSO.

FORESTRY COMMISSION. *Gwydyr Forest in Snowdonia.* 1971. HMSO.

FORESTRY COMMISSION. *Snowdonia National Forest Park.* 1954. HMSO.

HYDE, H. A. *Welsh Timber Trees.* 3rd ed. 1961. National Museum of Wales.

GEOLOGY

NORTH, F. J. *The Slates of Wales.* 1925. University of Wales Press.

SMITH, B. and GEORGE, T. N. *British Regional Geology: North Wales.* 3rd ed. 1961. HMSO.

INDUSTRY

CHRISTIANSEN, R. and MILLER, R. W. *The Cambrian Railways* (2 vols.). 1967. David and Charles.

JENKINS, T. G. *The Welsh Woollen Industry.* 1969. National Museum of Wales.

LEE, C. E. *The Welsh Highland Railway.* 1971. David and Charles.

REES, D. M. *Mines, Mills and Furnaces.* 1969. National Museum of Wales.

LOCAL HISTORY

BOWEN, E. G. and GRESHAM, C .A. *History of Merioneth.* 1967. Merioneth Historical and Record Society.

NATURAL HISTORY

LACEY, W. S. (ed.) *Welsh Wildlife in Trust.* 1970. North Wales Naturalists' Trust.

LOCKLEY, R. M. *The Naturalist in Wales.* 1970. David and Charles.

PLACE NAMES

DAVIES, E. (ed.) *A Gazetteer of Welsh Place Names,* 1967. University of Wales Press.

WALKING AND CLIMBING

FORESTRY COMMISSION. *Walks in Gwydyr Forest.* 1971. HMSO.

JAMES, RON. *Rock Climbing in Wales.* 1970. Constable.

POUCHER, W. A. *The Welsh Peaks.* 3rd ed. 1967. Constable.

APPENDIX I

National Nature Reserves in the Snowdonia National Park

Sixteen reserves of the Nature Conservancy have (1971) been established in the Park. They are:

Cader Idris Includes the summit of the mountain and Llyn Cau.

[1]*Coed Camlyn* Near Maentwrog. Oak wood with bilberry, grass and mosses.

[2]*Coed Cymerau* In the upper Vale of Ffestiniog. Oak wood in a humid gorge.

[2]*Coed Dolgarrog* At Dolgarrog. Oak wood with Ash, Beech, Elm, and Alder.

Coed Ganllwyd At Ganllwyd. Oak wood and Rhaiadr Du Waterfalls with abundant ferns, mosses and liverworts.

[2]*Coed Gorswen* Near Ro Wen. Mixed oak wood relatively rich in flowering plants.

Coedydd Maentwrog Near Maentwrog. Oak wood with bracken and grasses.

[1]*Coed y Rhygen* West side of Trawsfynydd Reservoir. Oak and Birch wood with abundant mosses and liverworts.

[1]*Coed Tremadog* At Tremadog. Mixed woodland. Cliffs and scree.

[1]*Cwm Glas Crafnant* Near Crafnant Lake. Outcrop of calcareous rock with associated flowering plants and supporting Ash, Birch, Hazel and Hawthorn woodland.

Cwm Idwal Pass of Nant Ffrancon. Mountain plant communities, interesting geological features and many striking evidences of the Ice Age.

[1]*Morfa Dyffryn* Between Harlech and Barmouth. Sand dunes.

[1]*Morfa Harlech* Near Harlech. Sand flats, salt marsh and dunes.

Rhinog Includes the top of Rhinog Fawr mountain. Rugged terrain with dense heather.

Snowdon-Yr Wyddfa Wide range of habitats from the oak woods near Llyn Dinas to the windswept sub-arctic heaths at over 3,000 feet.

Dyfi (part) An extensive reserve including mudflats, salt marsh, sand dunes and peatlands of geomorphological, botanical and ornithological interest.

A permit is required for wildfowling. Apply to the Regional Officer for South Wales, Plas Gogerddan, Aberystwyth.

For further references see text.

[1]Permit required to enter the Reserve. At Morfa Dyffryn, for only parts of the Reserve.

[2]Permit required to visit away from public footpaths or rights of way in the Reserve.

Application for permits, stating the dates for which the permit is required, should be made to the Regional Officer for North Wales, Nature Conservancy, Penrhos Road, Bangor.

L

APPENDIX II

Landscape Trails in the Snowdonia National Park

Name of Trail	Approximate Length	Map Reference
(a) Set up by Snowdonia Park Joint Advisory Committee:		(O.S. 1″ scale)
Precipice Walk	3 mile circuit on the 800 foot contour line	SH 743212
Cefn Isa Farm Trail	2 mile circuit from Salem Chapel, Llanbedr	SH 603273
Nantcol Nature Trail	¼ mile circuit from car park in Cwm Nantcol	SH 605270
Gwern Gof Uchaf Farm Trail	Access from A5 E., N., and W. of Gwern Gof Uchaf farmhouse	SH 672602

Plaques along trails—no leaflet required.

(b) Forestry Commission Trails:		
Beddgelert Forest Trail	1 mile	SH 576495
Gwydyr Forest Trail	3 miles	SH 755575
Lady Mary's Walk	1 mile circuit from Gwydir Castle	SH 797610
Ty'n y Groes Forest Trail	2 mile or 1 mile circuit	SH 725232
Dolgefeiliau Forest Trail	Circuits varying from ½ to 2 miles	SH 721265
Tan y Coed Forest Trail	2 mile or 1 mile circuit	SN 758055

Leaflets available from the District Officers at Gwydyr Uchaf, Llanrwst, Denbighshire, or Smithfield St., Dolgellau, Merioneth; the National Park Information Officer, Yr Hen Ysgol, Maentwrog, Blaenau Ffestiniog, Merioneth; or National Park Information Centres.

(c) Nature Conservancy Trails:		
Coed Llyn Mair Nature Trail	1 mile circuit	SH 651413
Cwm Idwal Nature Trail	2 mile circuit	SH 602650
Cwm y Llan Nature Trail	2 miles	SH 624503
Miners' Track	2 miles	SH 644554

Leaflets available from the Regional Officer, Nature Conservancy, Penrhos Road, Bangor, Caernarvonshire; the National Park Information Officer, Yr Hen Ysgol, Maentwrog, Blaenau Ffestiniog, Merioneth; or National Park Information Centres.

APPENDIX III

Scheduled Ancient Monuments in the Snowdonia National Park

(The parish name appears first)

BURIAL MOUNDS AND MEGALITHIC MONUMENTS

	1 in. O.S. Sheet *Grid Reference*
Aber, Carnedd y Saeson and neighbouring cairns N.W. of Foel Dduarth	SH 679718
Caerhun, Barclodiad y Gawres round cairn	SH 716717
Caerhun, Bwlch y Ddeufaen standing stones	SH 715718
Caerhun, Cerrig Pryfaid stone circle	SH 724713
Caerhun, Porth Llwyd burial chamber	SH 770677
Cerrigydrudion, Cae Garn round barrow	SH 890473
Conwy M.B. and Henryd, Hafotty standing stone	SH 747749
Gyffin, Cefn Llechen stone circle	SH 747755
Henryd, Maen Penddu	SH 739736
Llanaber, Carneddau Hengwm long cairns	SH 614206
Llanbedr, standing stones	SH 584269
	SH 608321
Llandanwg, Moel Goedog round cairns and standing stones	to
	SH 611325
Llanddwywe-is-y-graig, Corsygedol burial chamber	SH 603228
Llanddwywe-is-y-graig, Llecheiddior round cairn	SH 612220
Llandecwyn, Bryn Cader Faner round cairn	SH 648353
Llandecwyn, Llyn Eiddew Bach round cairns	SH 642346
Llandecwyn, Y Gyrn round cairn	SH 641358
Llanegryn, group of standing stones 900 yards S.W. of Bryn Seward	SH 617113
Llanegryn, two round cairns and two standing stones,	SH 634120
Bryn Seward	and SH 624117
Llanenddwyn, Bron y Foel west burial chamber	SH 609245
Llanenddwyn, Dyffryn burial chamber	SH 589228
	SH 599309
Llanfair, Fonlief Hir standing stones	to
	SH 601314
Llanfair, Gwern Einion burial chamber	SH 587286
Llangelynnin, Llynnau Cregennen standing stone	SH 662138
Llanrwst, Maen Pebyll burial chamber	SH 844566
*Llanrwst Rural, Capel Garmon burial chamber	SH 818544
Llanuwchllyn, cairn 250 yards S. of Moel Caws	SH 845273
Maen y Bardd burial chamber	SH 741718
Tywyn, Tarcn Hendre cairn	SH 683039
Trawsfynydd, Llech Idris	SH 732311

STONE ROWS AND CISTS

Pentrefoelas, Cefn y Gadfa stone rows and cists	SH 878935
Pentrefoelas, Hafod y Dre stone rows	SH 885537

CAMPS AND ANCIENT SETTLEMENTS

Aber, Foel Dduarth enclosure	SH 681716
Aber, hut group 830 yards S.E. of Bod Silin	SH 678722
Aber, hut group W. of Foel Dduarth	SH 677716
Aber, hut group 200 yards N.W. of Hafod y Gelyn	SH 675715
Aber, Maes y Gaer	SH 663725
Beddgelert, Cwm Dyli ancient village	SH 655542
Beddgelert, Dinas Emrys	SH 604492
Beddgelert, Pen y Gaer	SH 586458
Brithdir, Roman fort	SH 772189
Brithdir and Islaw'rdref, Tyddyn y Coed camp	SH 694158
Caerhun, early fields and dwellings near Maen y Bardd	SH 741720
Caerhun, Pant y Griafolen huts and enclosures	SH 708666
Capel Curig, Bryn y Gefeiliau ancient village	SH 749573
Clynnog, Caerau ancient village	SH 469490
Conwy, Castell Caer Lleion	SH 757778
Dolbenmaen, Castell Caerau	SH 509439
Dolbenmaen, Llyn Cwm Ystradllyn hut circle	SH 560440
Henryd, Caer Bach	SH 744730
Henryd, hut groups N. of Cerrig y Dinas	SH 753742
Henryd, round hut 80 yards S. of St. Celynin's church	SH 751737
Llanaber, Pen y Dinas camp	SH 606208
Llanbedrycennin, Pen y Gaer	SH 750694
Llandanwg, Muriau'r Gwyddelod ancient village	SH 586303
Llandanwg, Talsarnau and Llanfair, Moel Goedog camp	SH 614325
Llanddwywe-is-y-graig, Craig y Dinas	SH 624230
Llanenddwyn, Berth Ddu hut circles	SH 592228
Llanenddwyn, Byrllysg camp	SH 597241
Llanfachreth, Moel Offrwm camp	SH 750210
Llanfachreth, Moel Offrwm lower camp	SH 750206
Llanfairfechan Dinas	SH 701739
Llanfairfechan, Gwern y Plas ancient village	SH 687748
Llanfihangel-y-Pennant and Tywyn, Craig yr Aderyn hill-fort	SH 644068
Llangelynnin, Castell-mawr camp	SH 579049
Llangelynnin, Castell y Gaer	SH 592090
Llangelynnin, huts 450 yards S.S.E. of Mynydd Graig Wen	SH 616115
Llangelynnin, Tal y Gareg camp	SH 573036
Llanllechid, early fields and dwellings E. of Llanllechid	SH 631686
Llanllechid, huts 100 yards N. of Cil Twllan	SH 636665
Llanllechid, huts and enclosures in Cwm Caseg	SH 658670
Llanllechid, huts and enclosures S.E. of Glan Llugwy	SH 692606
Llanllechid, Rhiw Goch camp	SH 616693
Llanuwchllyn, hut group and enclosures 130 yards S. of Moel Caws	SH 845274
Trawsfynydd, hut groups S. of Bwlch y Ffordd	SH 721281

ROMAN REMAINS

Capel Curig, Bryn y Gefeiliau Roman site	SH 747573
Llanuwchllyn, Caer Gai	SH 877315

Maentwrog, Tomen y Mur	SH 706387
Pennal, Cefn Gaer Roman site	SH 705001
Trawsfynydd, Dol-ddinas Roman earthworks	SH 735378
Trawsfynydd, Roman kilns 250 yards S.E. of Pen y Stryd	SH 728319

INSCRIBED STONES

Dolbenmaen, Gesail-gyfarch inscribed stone	SH 541418
Ffestiniog, Roman inscribed stones at Plas Tanybwlch	SH 655406
Talsarnau, inscribed stone in Llanfihangel-y-traethau churchyard	SH 595354

ECCLESIASTICAL BUILDINGS

*Llanelltyd, Cymer Abbey	SH 721195
*Llanrhychwyn, Gwydir Uchaf chapel	SH 795610

CASTLES

Aber castle mound	SH 656727
Bala, Tomen y Bala castle mound	SH 928361
Dolbenmaen castle mound	SH 506430
*Dolwyddelan Castle	SH 722524
*Llanberis, Dolbadarn Castle	SH 586598
*Llandanwg, Harlech Castle	SH 581312
Llanegryn, Domen Dreiniog	SH 596037
*Llanfihangel-y-Pennant, Castell y Bere	SH 667086
Llanfor, Pen-ucha'r-llan ringwork	SH 938368
Llangower, Castell Gronw castle mound	SH 930350
Llanuwchllyn, Castell Carndochan	SH 847306
Pentrefoelas, Y Foelas castle mound	SH 870523
Pentrefoelas, Maes Gwyn castle mound	SH 864524
Tywyn, Tomen Las castle mound	SH 697003
Trawsfynydd, Castell Prysor	SH 758368

OTHER SECULAR SITES AND BUILDINGS

Aber, medieval homestead 430 yards S.E. of Maes y Gaer	SH 666724
Llangelynnin, Llys Bradwen medieval site	SH 650139
Penmachno, barn N. of Pen y Bryn	SH 787503
Penmachno, Fedw Deg old house	SH 789533

BRIDGES

Aber, Bontnewydd	SH 662720
Betws y Coed, Pont y Pair	SH 792567
Dolgellau Bridge	SH 728179
Ffestiniog, Pont Dolymoch	SH 685417
Llanbedr, Pont Llanbedr	SH 585268
Llanelltyd Bridge	SH 718193
Llanfachreth, Bontnewydd	SH 771201
Llanycil, Pont Tai-hirion old bridge	SH 803398
Penmachno, Pont Rhyd Lanfair	SH 828524
Pentrefoelas, Pont Newydd (northern)	SH 862513
Pentrefoelas, Pont Newydd (southern)	SH 862513

Note: The scheduling of an ancient monument does not imply public access. Certain monuments are however in the care of the Secretary of State for Wales and access to * these is permitted.

Index

The Country Code

GUARD AGAINST FIRE RISKS

Plantations, woodlands and heaths are highly inflammable: every year acres burn because of casually dropped matches, cigarette ends or pipe ash.

FASTEN ALL GATES

Even if you found them open. Animals can't be told to stay where they're put. A gate left open invites them to wander, a danger to themselves, to crops and to traffic.

KEEP DOGS UNDER PROPER CONTROL

Farmers have good reason to regard visiting dogs as pests; in the country a civilised town dog can become a savage. Keep your dog on a lead wherever there is livestock about, also on country roads.

KEEP TO PATHS ACROSS FARM LAND

Crops can be ruined by people's feet. Remember that grass is a valuable crop too, in some cases the only one on the farm. Flattened corn or hay is very difficult to harvest.

AVOID DAMAGING FENCES, HEDGES AND WALLS

They are expensive items in the farmer's economy; repairs are costly and use scarce labour. Keep to recognised routes, using gates and stiles.

LEAVE NO LITTER

All litter is unsightly, and some is dangerous as well. Take litter home for disposal; in the country it costs a lot to collect it.

SAFEGUARD WATER SUPPLIES

Your chosen walk may well cross a catchment area for the water supply of millions. Avoid polluting it in any way. Never interfere with cattle troughs.

PROTECT WILD LIFE, WILD PLANTS AND TREES

Wild life is best observed, not collected. To pick or uproot flowers, carve trees and rocks, or disturb wild animals and birds, destroys other people's pleasure as well.

GO CAREFULLY ON COUNTRY ROADS

Country roads have special dangers: blind corners, high banks and hedges, slow-moving tractors and farm machinery or animals. Motorists should reduce their speed and take extra care, walkers should keep to the right, facing oncoming traffic.

RESPECT THE LIFE OF THE COUNTRYSIDE

Set a good example and try to fit in with the life and work of the countryside. This way good relations are preserved, and those who follow are not regarded as enemies.

An illustrated booklet in colour is obtainable free from the Countryside Commission, 1 Cambridge Gate, Regent's Park, London, NW1 4JY.

Printed in England for Her Majesty's Stationery Office by
Wells KPL Swindon Press, Swindon, Wilts
Dd 503629 K100 6/74

Other illustrated Guides in the National Park Series

Brecon Beacons	**50p**	(57p)
Dartmoor	**40p**	(47p)
Exmoor	**42½p**	(51p)
Lake District (*New edition in course of preparation*)		
Northumberland	**37½p**	(45p)
North York Moors	**38p**	(46½p)
Peak District	**45p**	(52p)
Pembrokeshire Coast	**75p**	(83½p)
Yorkshire Dales	**45p**	(52p)

Prices in brackets include postage

Free lists of titles (please specify subject/s) are available from Her Majesty's Stationery Office, PM1A (ZS), Atlantic House, Holborn Viaduct, London EC1P 1BN.

Government publications can be bought from the Government bookshops in London (post orders to PO Box 569, SE1 9NH), Edinburgh, Cardiff, Belfast, Manchester, Birmingham and Bristol, or through booksellers.

 HMSO BOOKS